T0083688

Writers of Wales

Geoffrey of Monmouth

Editors:
Meic Stephens
Jane Aaron
M. Wynn Thomas

Honorary Series Editor:
R. Brinley Jones

Other titles in the Writers of Wales series:

Writers of Wales

Geoffrey of Monmouth

Karen Jankulak

University of Wales Press

Cardiff 2010

Reprinted 2011 (twice)

www.uwp.co.uk

British Library Cataloguing-in-Publication Data
A catalogue record for this book is available from the British Library.

ISBN 978-0-7083-2151-5
e-ISBN 978-0-7083-2314-4

Printed in England by CPI Antony Rowe, Chippenham and Eastbourne

Contents

Acknowledgements

I would like give profound thanks to John Carey and Oliver Padel, both of whom read a penultimate draft of this book. Any failure to take their very helpful suggestions, and any remaining errors are of course my own. I would like to thank Professor Brynley Roberts for his generous encouragement. I would like to thank the anonymous readers for University of Wales Press for valuable suggestions, and would like to particularly thank Sarah Lewis for her great patience. I would also like to thank Dawn Evans and Michelle Evans, without whose friendship and support I would not have been able to write this book. I would like to thank Jonathan Wooding, who read numerous drafts and encouraged me throughout in every possible way. Finally, I would like to dedicate this book to the late Gwenaël Le Duc, with profound appreciation for encouragement, much practical assistance and illuminating and stimulating conversations on a number of subjects, this last one cruelly cut short.

The chapter and line divisions of ed. Actom Griscom, *The Historia Regum Britanniae of Geoffrey of Monmouth* (London and New York: Longmans & Co., 1929) have been followed in this book. The author and publisher gratefully acknowledge the permission granted by the following to reprint extracts from:

Michael D. Reeve and Neil Wright (ed. and trans.), *Geoffrey of Monmouth. The History of the Kings of Britain* (Woodbridge: The Boydell Press, 2007).
Reproduced by permission of Boydell and Brewer Ltd.

Introduction

Geoffrey of Monmouth's *Historia Regum Britanniae*, 'The History of the Kings of Britain', was and is one of the most popular texts of the Middle Ages. Completed by 1139, it presented for the first time a coherent and detailed story of the early history of the British. This history stretched from the foundation of Britain to the decisive establishment of the Anglo-Saxons as rulers of England, taking in the foundation of Brittany along the way. Geoffrey's version of British history had a profound influence on historians into the modern period, one that persists to this day. This extends well beyond what is probably Geoffrey's best-known contribution to history: that is, the embryo of our familiar narrative of King Arthur. Geoffrey's inventiveness also gave us, among other things, Shakespeare's Lear, the term *Cambria* for Wales and, at least to a large extent, the figure we know as Merlin. In more general terms, Geoffrey introduced 'Britain' itself, a concept already familiar to the Welsh, to English historiography, and in doing so permanently affected the way English writers thought about Britain and its constituent regions. In a time when Wales was approaching the form that it has today, Geoffrey, while not clearly locatable, is a writer who draws upon and develops what came to be seen as the 'Welsh' tradition.

The Anglo-Saxon world had historians and biographers such as Bede and Asser well before the coming of the Normans; such detailed narratives are lacking for British history until the arrival of Geoffrey. Geoffrey's great strength was in presenting a complete story from beginning to end; his text resembles, at least superficially, what we as a modern audience think of as a narrative history.

In terms of factual accuracy his work is very far from what we would call 'history'. From the modern historian's point of view Geoffrey's writings have served less to inform us about Britain's early history than to provide tantalizing suggestions of what his manifold sources might have said, truly or falsely, about his subject matter. Writing true accounts about real events, however, wasn't Geoffrey's intention. The *Historia Regum Britanniae* is pre-eminently a story, and one with an overall literary and thematic unity. It is a lively and imaginative work, full of incident, stressing actions over what we might consider 'characterization' – its cast of characters, lacking personalities or self-reflection, serve instead to push along the unfolding events. The relentless march of 'history' dominates: each event, no matter how unhistorical, succeeds its predecessor in a relentlessly chronological framework. This is even more striking when we compare Geoffrey's Arthurian setting to that of the later romance tradition, which, despite its debt to Geoffrey or his vernacular translators, places its characters in a timeless setting dominated by personalized, often introspective, behaviour. Nevertheless, in terms of Arthurian studies, Geoffrey's work is the bridge between our fragmentary Welsh, Cornish and Breton Arthur, and via Wace and the romances, the Arthur of Thomas Malory, who forms the basis of the Arthur we most remember today.

Two writers, Gildas (sixth century) and the anonymous author of the *Historia Brittonum* (early ninth century), provide undoubted evidence of a historical consciousness in Britain prior to the Norman period. To their writings we can add the keeping of the Welsh annals and the compiling of genealogical collections, both well underway by the tenth century. We should further note that the biographer of Alfred the Great, Asser, was a Welshman by birth, educated at St Davids. Most surviving written materials in Wales are datable to the Norman and post-Norman period. This is not to say that these materials are 'Norman' rather than 'Welsh': in some cases the Norman presence in Wales or on its borders provided an impetus for writing down important accounts. In some cases the Normans did the copying or composing themselves. There is a wider context: the twelfth century in particular saw an explosion in the production of written accounts of contemporary history in

Norman England, often with a perceptible interest in the pre-Norman past. In this sense, Geoffrey is typical of his period and he is often treated as one of the relatively numerous Norman writers who are seen primarily as rooted in a universal, western European literary culture, rather than a specific regional or political context. While it is true that Geoffrey is very much at home in the mainstream of western European medieval writing, he can and should be considered within a Welsh context.

In one very significant sense Geoffrey was unusual. He moved well beyond the dipping in and out of pre-Saxon British history characteristic of other Norman writers or collectors, such as William of Malmesbury or the compilers of the manuscript known as *Vitae Sanctorum Wallensium* (British Library Cotton Vespasian A.xiv). Geoffrey was particularly interested in British history. He was, moreover, notably uninterested in Anglo-Saxon history. Geoffrey, uniquely, concerned himself exclusively with the distant, pre-Saxon, British past. This was possible, as less inventive contemporaries pointed out, because British history had been, until then, sparsely served by narrative histories. Geoffrey had apparently unearthed sources that had hitherto resisted discovery by their combined diligence, to their surprise or suspicion. Where Geoffrey got this material has long been a source of argument. Nevertheless, Geoffrey insisted on a British past that was every bit as sophisticated as the Roman or, by implication, Saxon or Norman past. In this Geoffrey stands alone among his contemporaries. Moreover, this defence of the British past contrasts with, or perhaps complements, an apparent lack of the overt political pleading that was characteristic of the era.

That Geoffrey defies classification among contemporary Norman historians is to a large extent due to his remaining faithful to themes that run strongly through the Welsh writings about history in the Middle Ages. Brynley Roberts has discussed Geoffrey's debt to medieval Welsh historiographical tradition – this brought a much-needed specialist view to the more generalized picture of Geoffrey as a Latin-language writer. To borrow a distinction used by medieval writers of romance, we can say that Roberts has shown that while Geoffrey took liberties with the *matière*, the people and events of his sources, he did not do so with regards to the *sens*, the overall meaning lying behind them. He was not simply a copier of the Welsh material, but an interpreter within the spirit of the Welsh tradition. Whatever his own 'ethnic' origins, this sensibility makes Geoffrey very much a Welsh writer. Moreover, regardless of the universality of Geoffrey's appeal, it is arguable that Geoffrey was writing specifically, although not exclusively, for a Welsh audience, including at least some material that would be intelligible only to those familiar with Welsh language and tradition. Fourteen years after Geoffrey was celebrated in an excellent volume by Michael Curley in the series Twayne's English Authors it is appropriate that he should here take his place among the Writers of Wales.

Geoffrey of Monmouth and His Work

William the Conqueror took the English throne in 1066. By the early decades of the twelfth century, when Geoffrey wrote his *Historia Regum Britanniae*, England had been ruled by Norman kings for more than seventy years. The process of establishing Norman rule was a long one, aided by many powerful Norman and Breton barons. This process was hindered by rebellions (particularly in the north), but by 1075 England was solidly under the authority of the Normans, with its significant English leaders neutralized or dead and their lands redistributed. Subsequent interruptions to Norman rule would come from amongst the Normans themselves and their supporters.

Wales was a different matter. Wales comprised numerous small 'kingdoms' that came to be dominated by three by the late eleventh century: Gwynedd, Powys and Deheubarth. Generally speaking, until the eleventh century the rulers of even the smaller kingdoms (such as Ceredigion) were referred to in Welsh as *brenin* (singular) or *brenhinoedd* (plural), 'kings', sometimes rendered in Latin as *rex* or *reges*. With the death of Rhys ap Tewdwr, king of Deheubarth, in 1093, the Anglo-Norman chronicler John of Worcester stated that, 'kings ceased to rule in Wales'; several versions of the Welsh annals known as *Brut y Tywysogion*, 'Chronicle of the Princes', seem to agree that this was a defining moment, noting at Rhys's death that 'yna y dygwydawd teyrnas y Brytanyeit' (then the dominion of the Britons fell). While we still find references after this to kings in both Welsh and Latin texts during the twelfth century, its meaning seems to have become devalued, with *princeps Wallie*, 'prince of Wales', becoming the title used for the most important of the Welsh rulers.

It is difficult to generalize, however, as *brenin* continued to be used even into the thirteenth century in a broadly political sense for a head of state, as distinct from the holder of a particular franchise.

Whatever we call them, the fact of the multiplicity of rulers and courts was extremely important in the political, military and literary culture of Wales. The prince's court (*llys*) was the venue of social, literary, military and governmental business. There would have been a large number of places for the court to assemble, some fixed, some occasional. The three largest kingdoms, Gwynedd, Powys and Deheubarth, had 'chief courts' at Aberffro, Mathrafal and Dinefwr respectively, but there would have been many smaller places to hold court as well. Several great courts stand out in our historical records: one, later (and somewhat anachronistically) described as the first eisteddfod, was held in 1176 by Rhys ap Gruffudd at Cardigan with competitions between poets and musicians. *Brut y Tywysogion* grandly claimed that it had been 'proclaimed a year before it was held throughout Wales and England and Scotland and Ireland and many other lands' ('a'r wled honno a gyhoedet ulwydyn kynn y gwneuthur ar hyt Kymry a Lloegyr a Phrydein ac Iwerddon a llawer o wladoed ereill'). The multiplicity of courts, large and small, fixed and moveable, provided one, perhaps the main, context for important literary activity, activity that concerned itself with commenting on the polit-ical, historical and cultural past and present of Wales. The medieval Welsh laws describe, among the list of regular officers of the court and unattached 'additional' officers, two kinds of professional poets. Among the additional officers is the *pencerdd*, 'the chief poet': he was not a regular member of the court and it is clear that he earned his living by moving from place to place, praising, as was his remit, the prince of the court or, if he could not do so (presum-ably as he had not been paid to do so), a prince of another court. The second type, the *bardd teulu*, 'household poet', and as his title suggests a regular member of the court, sang songs of an unspeci-fied type after the *pencerdd* had done – presumably this was less politically loaded entertainment. We have approximately 12,700 lines of poetry emanating from these poets (known, collectively, as *Beirdd y Tywysogion*, 'Poets of the Princes'), furnishing ample proof that poets would sing songs of praise to several rulers, assessing each one in terms of their conformity to a list of praiseworthy attributes and, more importantly for our benefit, making reference to a pool of events and archetypes from Britain's heroic past.

Thus these multiple courts and poets provided a powerful expression of a significant cultural unity, despite political fragmentation. For our purposes, it is important that they would also have provided a context for the development of a multiplicity of versions of essentially the same cultural artefacts. When we come to other types of literary activity, we can only speculate as to their audience and its setting. The medieval tale *Math uab Mathonwy* implies that itinerant storytellers also provided entertainment at a prince's court: this suggests that we might extend what we know about the performance of praise poetry to other literary genres. It may even be that these were practised by the same people. The nature, however, of the relation of stories such as *Math* to reality is an extremely complicated one. The further question of the relationship of other types of literary activities, the keeping of genealogical collections, the compilation of mnemonic tools (such as 'triads', lists of important events and characters grouped in threes), to this court-centred poetry and storytelling, can only be a matter of conjecture. The extent to which the keeping of monastic annals, first in Latin from the eighth century or perhaps earlier, and then later in Welsh from the thirteenth century, formed a part of this activity is also a matter for debate. Finally, the circumstances under which someone like Geoffrey might have had sustained access to the wide range of material to which he undoubtedly did have access (directly or through an intermediary) is obscured by our inability to be sure of exactly who was producing it, and for whom. What we can say is that Geoffrey was acutely aware of the cultural unity of the Welsh material, marshalling it into an overall 'British' history with a vengeance.

With its multiplicity of political units, medieval Wales was extremely diverse and this had implications for both domestic and foreign politics. Each ruler would exert as much autonomy and claim as much overlordship as he could manage. The various ruling dynasties were often closely related and could be periodically

7

united under one ruler. Not the least of the challenges to political stability was the ruler's own family, whose potential claim to rule led to near constant infighting, sometimes with brutal results (although it is debatable whether this was more brutal than other contemporary societies). The Norman kings of England mostly left Wales to their barons to conquer as they wished, taking very little direct interest until the thirteenth century. There were many reverses: Gwynedd, for example, was overrun in the last decades of the eleventh century but by the beginning of the twelfth century regained its former independent status, one that it would keep until the late thirteenth century. It would be the last independent region of Wales to fall to the English. By the beginning of the twelfth century most of southern Wales (especially the south-east) was subject to Norman rule, with the king of England, the theoretical overlord of many of these areas, paying relatively little attention unless his barons there misbehaved. The Normans, then, added yet another element to the complex and decentralized political arena that was medieval Wales. The delegation of power to the barons in outlying areas effectively added to the already patchwork nature of Wales.

Politics were equally complicated in the wider Norman world. In 1120, the Norman king of England, Henry I, lost his only legitimate son and male heir. This set the stage for civil war. After his death in 1135, Henry's nephew Stephen took up the crown but was challenged after 1138 by Henry's daughter Matilda, the wife of Geoffrey of Anjou (and formerly the wife of the Holy Roman Emperor Henry V, hence her epithet 'empress'). This conflict, which lasted until the accession of Matilda's son Henry II in 1154, enlisted the powerful Norman and Breton barons on either side, resulting in a pattern of different – and at times shifting – political loyalties. It might be noted that Robert, earl of Gloucester, Geoffrey's chief patron and one of the dedicatees of the *Historia*, was one of Matilda's chief supporters.

Needless to say, the fact that the Norman kings and barons were preoccupied with the civil war was quickly taken advantage of by the other polities subject, or partially subject, to the Normans, chiefly the Scots and the Welsh. Welsh revolts brought about a dramatic Norman retreat in the south of Wales, in the border, and in north-east Wales. Successes against the Normans did not mean that dynastic tensions between the Welsh rulers themselves ceased, and the expansion of Gwynedd and, to a lesser extent, Powys during this period was achieved at the expense of both Norman and Welsh neighbours. Deheubarth, its ruling house having been almost extinguished under Henry I, rallied as well. Border areas were re-colonized by the Welsh.

Additionally, the Welsh could be called upon as allies by Norman factions, most often those supporting Matilda. Robert of Gloucester had Welsh allies among his troops. The Norman historian Orderic Vitalis commented on the bloodthirstiness of the Welsh or, as he termed them, *barbari*:

> they did not show consideration to holy places nor the reverence of religion, but persevered in pillage and burning and slaughter. I cannot relate each instance of the afflictions of the Church of God suffered by her sons who each day were butchered like cattle by the swords of the British (*Ecclesiastical History*, Bk xiii.41).

His comments were echoed by several other Anglo-Norman historians of the period, including the author of *Gesta Stephani* (Deeds of Stephen) and John of Worcester. Not content with retrenching, the Scots under David I pushed southwards into England, producing similar, but more detailed and heated, descriptions of their barbarity in warfare from these and other contemporary historians.

The incessant political conflict, inherent in decentralized regions such as Wales, and the sometimes undeniable savagery of its pursuit of power at the expense of numerous rivals seem to have led the Anglo-Norman historians to view as separate the 'barbarous' world of the Scots, the Welsh and later the Irish.

The accession of Henry II in 1154 marked the beginning of a very successful process of conquest, re-conquest and integration of the fringes of Henry's empire. Scotland, Wales, Brittany and parts of Ireland were brought firmly under Henry's rule. Laws and ecclesiastical structures were centralized and regularized. Native laws were gradually, often willingly, abandoned. The rulers of the kingdom of Scotland, much more unified than Wales, frequently achieved a status as fellow-rulers vis-à-vis the rulers of England.

This status was mainly denied the Welsh kingdoms. The numerous Welsh and Irish princes and their small kingdoms ultimately remained to be conquered: the Welsh not decisively until the late thirteenth century under Edward I; the Irish ultimately ignored, not to be taken up again until the Elizabethan period. Brittany's connections to the Angevins were decisively severed in the reign of King John, to the advantage of the Capetian kings of France.

Within this picture we try to place Geoffrey of Monmouth. This is difficult because we know relatively little about him. In all of his writings he described himself as Galfridus Monemutensis, 'Geoffrey of Monmouth'. There is general agreement that he was also the Geoffrey who witnessed seven charters concerning Oxford religious houses. The first five, dating from 1129 to c.1150, are signed by a cleric who called himself Galfridus Artur, 'Geoffrey Arthur'. Although it has been argued that 'Arthur' could have been Geoffrey's father's name, which might thereby suggest Welsh or, more probably, Breton origins, most scholars now agree that this is unlikely. An alternative is to consider it a nickname, inspired by Geoffrey's literary interests. Certainly his near-contemporaries Gerald of Wales and William of Newburgh used it in this fashion. It is interesting in this connection to see Geoffrey using it at least five years before the publication of any of his writings about Arthur. One gets the impression that he was inclined to talk about his interests and to accept that they were something of an obsession.

In one of the Oxford charters Geoffrey was described as *magister*, which suggests that he had pursued further studies, possibly on the continent. We can infer that Geoffrey moved to Oxford by 1129, as a teacher and probably one of the secular canons of the church of St George in Oxford Castle. In two further charters, dated to 1151, he was described as 'bishop' (prematurely) or 'bishop-elect' (more accurately) of St Asaph, a new bishopric in north-east Wales. According to the profession rolls of the Archbishopric of Canterbury, Geoffrey was ordained a priest on 16 February 1152 and consecrated bishop on 24 February of the same year. He is not known to have visited his see in the three remaining years of his life, being prevented, it would seem, by the struggles of Madog ap Maredudd and his sons to wrest Powys from Norman control. In

1153, Geoffrey (as bishop of St Asaph) was among the witnesses to the Treaty of Westminster which ended the civil war between Stephen and Henry II. According to the Welsh chronicle, *Brut y Tywysogion*, Geoffrey died in 1155; he is described, inexplicably, as 'bishop of Llandaff', presumably because St Asaph was as yet little known. What Nicholas ap Gwrgan, bishop of Llandaff from 1148, might have thought of this can only be imagined – at any rate, he wasn't to die until 1183, so it is not the case that Geoffrey was confused with him.

Two main strands emerge from what these sources tell us about Geoffrey. One concerns Oxford, and Geoffrey's friends and patrons there. Of these, the most important is Walter, archdeacon of Oxford (d.1151), who appears in three of the charters witnessed by Geoffrey and is named by him in *Historia Regum Britanniae* as the person who supplied him with 'a certain most ancient book in the British language'. The other strand concerns Monmouth, for which connection there is no evidence apart from Geoffrey's self-description in his literary works. In the *Historia*, Geoffrey took a great interest in Wales and in the area around Monmouth in particular. The best explanation is that this is where he was born. This is not a conclusive argument, however, as the area around Monmouth, Caerleon in particular, has obvious attractions in its extensive Roman remains as a setting for long-ago deeds. Geoffrey located Arthur's court in Caerleon, although previous Welsh tradition usually situated it in Cornwall: did this reflect his pride in his own origins? Did it reflect Geoffrey's interest in Britain's monumental past? The two need not be mutually exclusive.

Further cause for speculation is the fact that Monmouth in the late eleventh and early twelfth century was controlled by a Breton family rather than a Norman family. While this was not at all unusual, it has suggested a context for what some scholars have seen as the Breton sympathies or even sources of the *Historia*. If Geoffrey was indeed from Monmouth, it is possible that he was of Breton origin. He could have also been of Welsh origin. The fact that he has a Norman name, Galfridus, need not contradict this. However, the attempt to confirm Geoffrey's biographical details by trying to read into the *Historia*'s particular political and ethnic sympathies is a subjective process. Moreover, it is clear from surviving manuscripts that Normans could and did take a lively interest in the traditions of the areas that they conquered or tried to conquer. Whatever his relationship to the Welsh, it is clear that Geoffrey did more than use native British sources: he engaged with a living tradition and continued it in a meaningful way.

2

Historia Regum Britanniae and its Sources

Scholars have debated Geoffrey's intentions in writing the *Historia*, with reference to his purported background, his sympathies as shown in his writings and his faithfulness to his sources – or lack thereof. Therein lies a large problem: we must ask ourselves how much of the *Historia Regum Britanniae* is Geoffrey's invention, how much is 'traditional' material? How much, if any, does Geoffrey's distortion of his source material owe to his own vision of British history (and to what extent was this vision affected, moreover, by contemporary political machinations)? How much is due to the need to tell an exciting and coherent story? These questions also impact upon our assessment of Geoffrey's affiliations to tradition. How active was his engagement with his source material?

The question of Geoffrey's sources is very difficult. Geoffrey claimed in the dedication to the *Historia* (Bk i.1) to have translated 'a very old book in the British tongue' (*Britannici sermonis*), presented to him by 'Walter, archdeacon of Oxford'. At the end of the *Historia* he referred again to Walter and the book brought from 'Britain' (*ex Britannia*; Bk xii.20). Geoffrey described Walter as 'a man skilled in the rhetorical arts and in foreign histories' (Bk i.1) as well as 'a man very familiar with many histories' (Bk xi.1). Henry of Huntingdon also spoke of Walter's skill in writing Latin – he is not known to be connected with any 'British' material apart from Geoffrey's statement. The nature and identity of this supposed British source obviously bears greatly upon any interpretation of Geoffrey as a Welsh or Celtic writer. While scholarly trends have in the past at times taken Geoffrey's claim to have translated a British book seriously, the claim is now, however, mostly viewed as pure fiction. We should be aware that the claim to translate, or revise, older sources is a literary formula, sometimes used to give plausibility to the transmission of a mostly fictional story. It appears that Geoffrey was probably lying to cover up the fact that much of the *Historia* was his own invention. Was he more 'historical novelist' than historian then, a sort of medieval Walter Scott? Some readers, disappointed at the lack of historicity in much of Geoffrey's account of Arthur, would dismiss him in this way, but a closer look leads to a less simple explanation. It is clear that Geoffrey had sources, oral or written, in the British tradition, at least one that was probably overwhelmingly Welsh in origin. The existence of a comparable Breton tradition is also clear, although it is not so extensive in its surviving material and Geoffrey's particular debt to it is uncertain. We should note, as well, that 'British' could mean Welsh, Breton or even Cornish, and at any rate it is not clear that a contemporary audience would have distinguished between these. However, it should be noted that in all other instances, unless the context is already absolutely clear, Geoffrey was careful to distinguish Brittany from Britain in some fashion.

One Cambro-Latin text does stand out as Geoffrey's main source, though his work can in no way be regarded as a translation of its contents. *Historia Brittonum* ('History of the Britons') has often been attributed to Nennius, although his authorship is now significantly in doubt. Datable to the years 829/30, it originated in the court of Merfyn Frych, king of Gwynedd, which was known from other contemporary sources as an important staging-post of Irish clerics on their way to the continent, a fact supported in the materials presented in *Historia Brittonum*. In it, we have the earliest version of the legend of the founding of Britain by Brutus and the stage set for later events, especially those connecting Britain and Rome: all appear later in Geoffrey's *Historia Regum Britanniae*. *Historia Brittonum* is one of Geoffrey's main sources – it provided the basic framework of Geoffrey's *Historia* in terms of its beginning, some important events along the way and its approximate ending. Another significant source was *De Excidio Britanniae* ('On the Ruin of Britain'), written by the cleric Gildas probably in the mid-sixth century. Geoffrey knew this work very well, as did Gerald of Wales, a later Cambro-Norman historian, but notably unlike other Anglo-Norman historians living in the twelfth century, who either did not know or did not respect Gildas's writing. Geoffrey drew on *De Excidio Britanniae* liberally, sometimes copying it verbatim, frequently without attribution, which was not at all an uncommon procedure. Less common a procedure was Geoffrey's false attribution of stories to Gildas, something he did five of the seven times he cited him. This calculation takes into account the fact that Geoffrey refers to both the *De Excidio Britanniae* and the *Historia Brittonum* as the work of Gildas, probably because many manuscripts, erroneously, do so – Geoffrey's incorrect references to Gildas as an authority do not refer to *Historia Brittonum*. They are entirely invented.

Geoffrey also relied on the *Historia Ecclesiastica gentis Anglorum* ('Ecclesiastical History of the English People') of Bede (early eighth century), a text that, unlike Gildas's, was very well known amongst Geoffrey's Norman contemporaries. Geoffrey named Bede with approbation in his dedication, but cited him only once with respect to a specific matter, and then only to disagree with him (Bk xii.14). This is entirely in keeping with *Historia Regum Britanniae*'s profound challenge to Bede's view of British and English history, a challenge that William of Newburgh, one of Geoffrey's most vehement critics, held to have been won by Bede, as he stated in the preface to his *Historia Rerum Anglicarum*. But William was in the minority: English history until the sixteenth century followed Geoffrey's version, not Bede's. It may well be that Geoffrey's invention of his supposed older British source cast Bede, where he and Geoffrey disagreed, in the light of the inventor and adapter. While we are now indeed aware of Bede's own adaptations, it is clear that he was a very poor second to Geoffrey in terms of invention.

Also, Geoffrey clearly had access to a significant amount of Welsh genealogical material, although from what precise source we cannot be sure, as he seems to adapt it relatively freely. The most important, and earliest, collection of Welsh genealogical material, found alongside copies of *Historia Brittonum* and *Annales Cambriae* ('Welsh Annals'), is in the Harleian manuscript (British Library Harley MS 3859, *c.*1100, but the genealogical material probably dating to the tenth century). This is a surviving example of the sort of source Geoffrey might have used.

It is clear that Geoffrey made relatively free with the details of his sources, changing roles, adapting names of one character to another, combining and altering stories to suit his purpose. The extent to which he did this, and the extent to which he invented things altogether, are often not clear. Thus, when he tells a particular tale that seems to have a particular point, one is not sure whether he inherited or created the tale and its ostensible point. Medieval writers often borrowed directly or reshaped their sources in ways we would not freely do today, but Geoffrey is notable for how infrequently his precise sources can be identified. This suggests that a lot of the material was directly invented, or changed to the point of not being recognizable, or perhaps was based on sources that are no longer extant, keeping in mind how little medieval narrative material we have from Wales and the virtual absence of this from Brittany. That being said, we do not have evidence from Wales or Brittany that large numbers of texts did once exist but have not survived, such as we have, for example, from Ireland in the form of long lists of tales, many of which no longer exist.

We might not be surprised if Geoffrey freely adapted relatively obscure material which one might assume he believed could be altered without being challenged, especially if circulated amongst an audience unfamiliar with its original version. But Geoffrey could also be surprisingly bold in his inventions as regards much better-known material: one example is Geoffrey's 'Molmutine Laws'. According to Geoffrey, these laws, codified during the pre-Roman period, 'are still renowned even today among the English' (Bk ii.17). In fact, Geoffrey invented these laws and attributed them to a relatively obscure character, Dyfnwal Moelmud, whose name is found in tenth-century genealogical lists in a northern British context and whose position there would locate him in the early or mid-sixth century. Geoffrey may have been drawing on Welsh tradition in associating Dyfnwal with legislation: two thirteenth-century Welsh law books name him as an important early medieval legislator and minor differences suggest that they were drawing on other Welsh material in addition to Geoffrey's. Both Geoffrey and the law tracts associate Dyfnwal with Cornwall: this suggests that Geoffrey had access to information outside the genealogical lists alone. In this case, as is so often the case with Geoffrey's use of sources, there is considerable, probably permanent, disagreement as to the extent to which Geoffrey drew on, or contributed to, such 'traditional' material.

Thus far, we are dealing with relatively obscure material. But Geoffrey made a bolder claim: he said that 'the historian Gildas translated [the laws] from British into Latin, and King Alfred [translated] from Latin into English' (Bk iii.5). This is a claim much more easily challenged, referring to well-known figures albeit in ways that are in keeping, to a certain extent, with their reputations. While Gildas was known as an authority on penitential matters and monastic discipline, given what we know of his views the notion that he translated anything from Welsh into Latin is risible. King Alfred, likewise, was a prolific, and famous, translator and legislator, whose extant works, however, do not include translations of British laws. Here Geoffrey combined invention with well-known and named sources, and mixed them, seeming to disregard truth and perhaps even the appearance of truth. Geoffrey's further statement, that these laws were known among the English of his day, is a typical example of his obvious sense of mischief. The further career of these laws would no doubt amuse Geoffrey: they have gone on to gain respectability, after a fashion, being mentioned by Shakespeare in *Cymbeline* and featuring in the 'discovery' of supposedly medieval legal triads attributed to Dyfnwal Moelmud by the notable late eighteenth and early nineteenth-century antiquary, Edward Williams ('Iolo Morganwg'). Such is the force of Geoffrey's and Iolo's versions that even in the early twentieth century academics credited the existence of these laws – a habit that has now taken hold on the Internet.

It will be useful now to summarize the overall progress of Britain's history as presented in the *Historia Regum Britanniae*. The work begins with the origins of Britain, its foundation by Brutus, a survivor of the Trojan war. Geoffrey gave Brutus three sons, eponyms of the island and its constituent regions: Locrinus was the eponym of Loegria, England; Kamber was the eponym of Kambria, Wales; and Albanactus was the eponym of Albania, Scotland (Bk ii.1). The account of pre-Roman Britain describes various dynastic successions and crises, interspersed with comments on where this fits into a classical and biblical scheme of events. The narrative is dominated by accounts of the foundation and naming of important sites. The climax of this period is the conquest of Rome by a British prince, Belinus, who then returned to Britain (Bk iii.1–10). The next portion describes the conquest of Britain initiated by the Roman emperor Claudius Caesar, following on several attempts by Gaius Julius Caesar, which either ended in failure or in a success with little or no impact. Claudius, however, conquered Britain decisively and married his daughter to a British prince (Bk iv.15). More dynastic squabbles occurred, partly to do with internal British politics, partly to do with Roman politics. Over and over Britain is presented as a platform from which legitimate or less legitimate Roman rulers gained or regained the rule of Rome. Brittany was conquered and populated with Britons (Bk v.12–16). Finally, Rome withdrew her legions leaving the British to cope alone in the face of incursions from numerous barbarian invaders (Bk vi.3). The next portion concerns the coming of the Saxons after the fall of Rome: the British appealed to Brittany for help, and the Breton rulers from time to time supplied armies and filled the kingship of Britain. The British (albeit unusually obscure in his exact origins) prince Vortigern was instrumental in inviting the Saxons to assist him in his ambitions and to chase out other barbarian invaders, but this backfired as the Saxons then took over. A long section, originally probably separate (it has its own introduction and dedication), is devoted to relatively obscure 'prophecies' given to Vortigern by a boy, Merlin (Bk vii). The main prophecies begin with the story of a red dragon (the British) that would engage in a continual struggle with a white dragon (the Saxons); the prophecies are notably vague, but it seems that the Normans would vanquish the white dragon. The prophecies end in an apocalyptic flourish with the entire world destroyed. This scene is crucial to set the stage for what happens subsequently and, amongst other things, prefigures (as well as explaining) Arthur's eventual failure.

After the section devoted to Merlin's prophecies, Geoffrey described how a combined force of British and Bretons fought the

Saxons with reverses and advances on both sides until Arthur, with help from the Bretons, decisively defeated them as well as other barbarian invaders. Arthur then conquered the rest of Europe, held a grand court at Caerleon (Bk ix.12–20) and set off to conquer Rome, handing Britain over to his nephew Modred during his absence. Arthur was winning the war and was on the point of gaining Rome itself when he was called back by news of Modred's treachery. Arthur was mortally wounded at the battle of Camblan, and carried to the Isle of Avalon. His cousin Constantinus became king (Bk xi.2). After this Britain was increasingly subject to the Saxons, partly because the Saxons were stronger, partly because the British were quarrelsome and disunited. Most of the British fled to Brittany but appeals for help from Brittany eventually failed; the Bretons explained that they were tired of helping the feeble British. Finally, the last British prince, Cadualadrus, heard an angel telling him that the British were not to rule Britain any more, 'until the time should come which Merlin had foretold to Arthur'. The angel promised, however, that 'the British people would one day recover the island, when the prescribed time came' (Bk xii.17). Cadualadrus consulted King Alanus of Brittany, who then consulted several prophetic sources, which were found to agree with the angel. Cadualadrus's son and nephew, Ivor and Yni, made a half-hearted attempt at fighting the Saxons, but were foiled by plague, famine and civil war. At this point, Geoffrey states, they went from being called the British to being called the Welsh, which Geoffrey says derived from their leader Gualo, or from their queen Galaes, 'or [from] their decline'. This is both inconclusive and dismissive. The Saxons wisely avoided civil war and, eventually, under their King Athelstan, ruled well over a united nation (Bk xii.19).

This brief summary of *Historia Regum Britanniae* does not do justice to the sheer amount of incident and detail, which were carefully marshalled by Geoffrey into coherence. Its overall theme is that the sovereign nation of Britain has been overrun by both Romans and Anglo-Saxons, and although its sovereignty has been lost, it has not been forgotten. Even as the Anglo-Saxons submerge much of Britain under their rule, a rule that is ultimately legitimate if not unambiguously so, the British are reassured that their sovereignty would be regained, although under extremely obscure circumstances. It is striking that the culmination of the uneven process of Saxon domination was delayed until, apparently, the tenth century under Athelstan of Wessex – having finished his British history Geoffrey was content to leave large gaps in that of the Anglo-Saxons. The extent to which the British loss of sovereignty was merited and to which the Anglo-Saxon domination was justified varies in Geoffrey's account of the last years of British rule. Notably, the conversion of the Anglo-Saxons to Christianity, a decisive moment in Bedan views of Anglo-Saxon history, in the *Historia* degenerated into an account of atrocities on the part of Anglo-Saxon rulers against British monks. While it retained, implicitly, Bede's criticism of the British churchmen for their bigoted refusal to minister to the Anglo-Saxons, Geoffrey's version, far from stressing the crucial fact of the Anglo-Saxons' conversion, merely turned the story into yet one more battle lost or won, entirely glossing over what should have been the point of the story (Bk xi.13). Clearly, Geoffrey's interest in the Anglo-Saxons, and debt to their historiographical traditions, was variable. His interest in the main theme of medieval Welsh historiography, the theme of sovereignty, loss of sovereignty and hope of future regaining of sovereignty, however, was all-encompassing. In this, Geoffrey took up a theme that pervaded medieval Welsh historical writing, occurring in the earliest Welsh 'historical' (perhaps pseudo-historical would be a better description) text, *Historia Brittonum*.

In terms of theme and broad outline, *Historia Brittonum*, or something like it, was a major source for Geoffrey. *Historia Brittonum* was written in Latin, not in the vernacular, and it certainly does not 'set out in excellent style a continuous narrative of all their deeds from the first king of the Britons, Brutus, down to Cadualadrus, son of Caduallo' (Bk i.1), so it cannot be the 'ancient book in the British tongue' that Geoffrey claimed to have used. Probably there was no such book: the description fits Geoffrey's own book far better than it does any potential source; later historians often mistook translations of Geoffrey into Welsh for a Welsh source of Geoffrey for this reason. A comparison with *Historia Brittonum* does, however, allow us to see Geoffrey's work as standing within an older Welsh tradition.

Historia Brittonum is one of our most important sources for early medieval British history. It provides a description of Britain and an account of British origins and early history in a framework of events, peoples and places, significant to medieval British intellectual tradition. This framework found first in *Historia Brittonum* is extremely important: it dominates all historical and pseudo-historical, and most genealogical, activity in medieval Wales. Almost every piece of remotely 'historical' writing in Wales can be referred to or fitted into the schema of *Historia Brittonum*. Hugely important legends appear in it first, although often in notably brief form; these found their way into Geoffrey's *Historia Regum Britanniae* in embellished and often altered form – the change, however, was usually in the detail rather than in the point of the story. *Historia Brittonum*, however, is also a complex text, and often obscure. It is generally dated to the year 829, a date established from a computistical note in chapter 16, which reckons the number of years from the coming of the Saxons to the presumed year of composition, the fourth year of the reign of King Merfyn of Gwynedd, that is 829/30. The text's authorship is somewhat more complicated: of the thirty-five or so medieval manuscripts of the *Historia Brittonum*, five contain a preface naming its author as Nennius and giving an account of its sources and editorial method. The preface seems to date to the tenth century or, more likely, the eleventh century and is now mostly regarded as added to the text rather than forming part of the original. In discarding the preface we discard not only the named author but, more importantly, the preface's explanation of the somewhat eccentric nature of the *Historia Brittonum* as a more or less unedited and certainly uncritical 'heap' of source material. This has meant that other explanations for the text's fragmentary and miscellaneous character (however much one might discern thematic coherence on a very broad scale) have been sought and it is to the nature of early British historiography that we turn in order to establish the tradition in which Geoffrey was writing.

3

Geoffrey's Models: Thinking about History in Medieval Wales and Ireland

If we allow that *Historia Brittonum* is not merely a collection of sources randomly assembled, we should seek to identify if it has an overall rationale. To what genre might it belong? The insular genre of 'synthetic-' or 'pseudo-' history seeks to reconcile, or synchronize, different events from different historical traditions. Individual scholars use slightly different terms for this genre, and have slightly different definitions. One clear characteristic is that texts of this genre tend to combine numerous, often contradictory, sources into a 'harmonized' whole, at times less than harmoniously. *Historia Brittonum* strikes one as sitting on the less harmonious end of this scale. We might further distinguish, with Thomas Charles-Edwards, between two different although complementary trends. On the one hand, we have 'synthetic pseudo-history', which projects a national unity into a legendary past with recourse to a single ancestor, involves the assimilation of various strands of indigenous traditions and applies Christian learning to the whole. On the other hand, we have 'synchronistic pseudo-history', which can be defined as the articulation of a chronological relationship between different peoples. Both of these sub-genres contribute to texts such as *Historia Brittonum* as well as medieval Irish historiographical texts, the *Lebor Gabála Érenn* ('Book of the Taking of Ireland') and its associated materials. Yet, these messy, historically disreputable texts also have much in common with other more apparently sober and reliable national and ecclesiastical histories of the period, Gregory of Tours's *Historia Francorum* ('History of the Franks'), Paul the Deacon's *Historia Langobardum* ('History of the Lombards') and, of course, Bede's *Historia ecclesiastica gentis Anglorum*, all of which contain legendary materials and show an interest in origin legends. These medieval histories seek to synchronize their national histories with those of other peoples. These shared aims were signs of a corporate vision of history in early medieval Europe and we need to judge this vision on its own terms and not just for its superficial similarities and dissimilarities to what we now term 'history'.

Unlike classical historical thinking, which for the most part saw historical events as expressing a cyclical pattern or a tale of decline from a primitive golden age (a view that highly affected the Greek and Roman historians' view of, for example, the ancient Celts and druids), Judaeo-Christian historians saw history as a linear progression: a divinely ordained sequence from a beginning (the Creation) to an implied end. The Christian historical scheme superseded any found in classical histories although it needed to take into account these venerable and authoritative traditions. Chronological comparisons needed to show the Creation as the earliest event of *all* human time. The best-known of the earliest 'chronological' writers is Sextus Julius Africanus (third century AD), whose *Chronographiae* do not survive but were used by the Greek writer Eusebius of Caesarea (early fourth century BC) in his much more wide-ranging and immensely influential *Chronicon*. Made up of two parts, the *Chronicon* consisted of a 'Chronograph', an epitome of universal history covering ancient near eastern, Old Testament, Egyptian, Greek and Roman history. The second part, known as *Chronicorum canones* but often called merely the 'Chronicle', consisted of a series of chronological notes presented in columns, starting from the birth of Abraham and locating lists of rulers of the ancient nations in parallel columns. Eusebius's *Chronicon* is no longer extant, but the second part, the *Chronicorum canones*, was translated by St Jerome into Latin in the later fourth century. Jerome also inserted Roman material, and the resulting 'Chronicle' was extremely influential as the account of ancient world history against which most early medieval 'national' histories calibrated themselves.

A lack of agreed-upon chronological anchors was evident in the early period. Schemes reckoned variously by Olympiads, by dating from the foundation of Rome or by various administrative features of the Roman empire (dating by indiction or consulships). By the fifth century, however, the need to properly calculate the date of Easter for liturgical purposes, a complex problem involving reconciling the solar and lunar calendars, led to the search for a common, agreed, chronological anchor. Thus the dating from the Incarnation, or *Anno Domini* dating, emerged supreme (with continuing adjustments to its calculation). Bede stands out as an early adopter of *Anno Domini* dating, one reason for his enduring reputation as a reliable historian.

Modern scholarship has, for the most part, ceased examining medieval sources that speak of an even earlier, otherwise obscure historical period, such as pre-Roman, Roman and post-Roman Britain, primarily in terms of whether they are accurate historical records and has started to consider them in their own historical context. Every text has its own context, its own aims and shares in expectations of the genre to which it belongs. We would now not necessarily assume a clear-cut and self-evident distinction between, for example, Bede on the one hand and the authors of various pseudo-historical texts on the other. While the former might present fewer problems for the extraction of notices of events (although one still needs an awareness of the author's motives and contexts), the latter type is just as interesting in its own historical context. The challenge is to take a text on its own terms and as a whole, rather than as a repository of facts, some true, some false. The distinction between what is true and what is false is not the only question to be asked, and at the very least should not be the first to be asked of a text, rather than after questions about authorial or editorial intent, purpose, driving themes and genres.

Irish material dominates discussions of medieval Celtic historical and pseudo-historical tradition, but the Welsh material is in fact similar in type if not in quantity. The schema later found in *Lebor Gabála Érenn* is found set out in an early form in *Historia Brittonum*. What all this suggests is that in the late first millennium in Ireland and Wales there was a wider tradition of historiography of which only *Historia Brittonum* now bears contemporary witness. In both these traditions we can see that our medieval 'synthetic historian' drew upon a vast field of material, some of which he favoured as more authoritative than others. This can be seen most strikingly in the tales of origin of peoples, places and institutions, sometimes termed 'origin legends' or 'aetiological' narratives. The compilers of these synthetic texts did not always believe them to be literally true: we need to credit our medieval authors with sufficient sophistication to recognize and deploy familiar genres whose ideas can be both literal and symbolic.

When deciding where to apply the distinction between 'historical' and 'not historical' to texts such as the *Historia Brittonum* we must address epistemological questions about both our medieval and modern historians' relationship to their, and our, interpretative hypotheses. Moreover, Geoffrey of Monmouth's *Historia Regum Britanniae* is a good corrective to the notion that narrative coherence, as evinced, for example, by Bede, can be taken to equate to historical authority. As manuscript history shows, somewhat to our surprise, *Historia Brittonum* was also a popular work within a very much living tradition. The result is labyrinthine, inconsistent and entirely bewildering. In this respect it has, not surprisingly, been compared unfavourably with Geoffrey's *Historia Regum Britanniae*, the faults of which are of the opposite kind.

Pseudo-historical synthesizing texts such as *Historia Brittonum* and *Lebor Gabála Érenn* attempt to include as much information (at times relatively contradictory) within its framework as possible. *Historia Brittonum* itself contains a significant amount of Irish material, including two different accounts of Irish origins. One of these, we have already noted, is clearly related to that appearing later in *Lebor Gabála Érenn*. *Historia Brittonum* gives two different accounts of the coming of the Irish to Ireland. The first (ch. 13) tells of several successive and abortive invasions of Ireland: first the Irish, the *Scoti*, came from Spain; a second group was shipwrecked in Ireland, and then after many years returned to Spain; a third group made a disastrous attack on a glass tower in the middle of the sea from which only one ship escaped (much of this is strikingly reminiscent of the Arthurian poem *Preiddeu Annwn*). From this ship, the *Historia Brittonum* states, came the present inhabitants of Ireland. The text goes on to name some of the Irish who settled in Britain and the Isle of Man. The second account (ch. 14), relates 'what the Irish scholars have told me', and attaches Irish origins to events described in the Old Testament. According to this account, a Scythian nobleman, who was present at, but did not take part in, the pursuit of the children of Israel across the Red Sea, was expelled by the Egyptians because of this. He and his people wandered through Africa and Europe until they settled in Spain, whence they came to Ireland. Their entry into Ireland is given as 1,002 years after the crossing of the Red Sea.

There are instructive similarities and differences between the two accounts of Irish origins found in *Historia Brittonum*. The first is for the most part a scholarly construct, using native and foreign materials: much is made of the meaning of names, borrowed from various Irish and non-Irish (written) sources. The basic invasion framework gives flexibility to the accommodation of a number of different stories. The second account, however, tries to insert the Gaels into an imported historical framework, in a manifestly ecclesiastical context, using the notion of one main wandering ancestor. Here we have the search for the promised land, both connected to and paralleling the Exodus story; here we have a wandering ancestor, albeit unnamed, to compare with Brutus, the ancestor of the British according to the same text (Brutus is discussed at greater length in chapter 5 below). While *Historia Brittonum*'s account of the Scythian aspect of Irish origins is a commonplace of many medieval origin legends, the addition of an Egyptian context is unprecedented: this is probably, although not provably, connected to statements, circulating at the same time in continental manuscripts, that the ancestor of the Irish was Scota, Pharaoh's daughter. The Irish material's lack of interest in a Trojan past is also noteworthy: in these respects the Irish and British origin legends in *Historia Brittonum* are quite different. This is probably partly due to the fact that the Irish material originated in a country without a Roman past; hence it had a slightly different view of Rome and its inheritance, in historiographical terms, from its medieval British counterparts. Moreover, the author of *Historia Brittonum* was determined to locate the coming of the British to Britain far earlier than the coming of the Irish to Ireland – a scheme replicated by Geoffrey of Monmouth.

The indigenous pseudo-historical genre offers much for the interpretation of Geoffrey's inventive, synthesizing approach to history – that aspect of his approach that separates him from his more antiquarian, less inventive Norman contemporaries. We can see how this genre of synthetic history came to develop a framework to draw together, on a national scale, numerous familial and political groupings to produce a unity, one located in a distant, prehistoric past but also connected with the notable events and nations of a much wider world. It resembles clearly Geoffrey of Monmouth's *Historia Regum Britanniae* in its drawing together of different traditions of, at times, wildly divergent origins, its harmonizing of indigenous history with that of the wider world, its basis in a notion that its subject (on the one hand the Irish, on the other the British) was a unified people with a unified history, albeit one subject to vicissitudes. Above all, however, *Lebor Gabála Érenn* and Geoffrey's *Historia Regum Britanniae* have much in common in terms of the strength of their relative impacts on later tradition. Geoffrey's work is far more polished and consistent – indeed, that is its main recommendation to its medieval and modern audiences – but this should not blind us to the common elements.

Both *Historia Brittonum* and *Lebor Gabála Érenn* began from the creation of the world and clearly sought to produce a 'national' myth to rival those of Israel and Rome. While in its later, far more elaborate manifestations in *Lebor Gabála Érenn* the Irish material would lend itself to political propaganda, the very early Irish material appearing in *Historia Brittonum*, like the British origin-legend material in that same text, is clearly scholarly speculation about perceived national origins, rather than political propaganda on behalf of a particular dynasty. While *Historia Brittonum* clearly showed its own textual origins in the kingdom of Gwynedd, including much material specifically concerning Gwynedd and its dynasties, its account of British origins has no regional bias. This somewhat unexpected breadth of vision is characteristic of medieval Welsh tradition as a whole.

Medieval Wales, like medieval Ireland (as well as medieval Brittany, early medieval Scotland and perhaps early medieval Cornwall if we consider *Cornubia* to have been distinct from

Dumnonia), was notable for its political decentralization and fragmentation. The basic political unit was the relatively small
kingdom, and internal dissension and raiding seem to have been a
permanent fact of life. Yet the Welsh and Irish historical tradition,
made up of many disparate texts, has a 'national' thrust that mostly
transcends the immediate political context. In the case of the Welsh
material, this national ideal was attached, not to Wales itself, but to
the whole of the island of Britain. This British conception is one that
explains Geoffrey's focus.

4

Geoffrey's Welsh Inheritance: the Red Dragon and the Promise of Sovereignty

Thus far we have examined the broad conception of 'national' history that existed in early medieval Britain and Ireland and have identified some of the common themes that give it coherence. We should pause now to identify the themes whose presence served to identify Geoffrey, whatever his origins, as an essentially Welsh historian and indeed as the one who brought a strong narrative to British history. We have seen how broad our definition of historians must be when it comes to Welsh and Irish literature, and we have assigned, with some conjecture but also with some confidence, the duty of presenting and controlling the learned view of the past to a class of literate, almost certainly professional, scholars who plied their trade at the courts of the numerous powerful and less powerful princes of the kingdoms of medieval Wales. In texts of various (and at times unclassifiable) genres, such as *Trioedd Ynys Prydein* ('The Triads of the Island of Britain'), the eleven prose tales found in the two manuscripts containing the Mabinogion collection (as distinct from the four tales within this collection that make up the 'Four Branches of the Mabinogi' proper), poems such as *Armes Prydein* and *Lives of Saints*, we find a vision of British history consistent with that of *Historia Brittonum*. The first, and main, theme is that Britain is properly one island, a sovereign whole under, ideally, one rule. If this does not conform to any historical reality, past or present (although one could argue for an essential linguistic and perhaps broad cultural unity in the pre-Roman period), it nevertheless expresses a defining, if chiefly symbolic, aspiration. The second, and related, theme is that this sovereignty was lost through invasions: usually, although not always, oppressive of the native British. In this the Welsh historical tradition directly resembles the Irish one. Oppressive invasions, known as *gormesoedd* (singular *gormes*), can be historical or mythical. Rome figures highly, although ambivalently, as a source and target of invasion – we will discuss this in detail below. The third, also related, theme running through medieval Welsh writing is that of a prophesied renewal of this sovereignty.

These themes create a leitmotif of a story of loss of sovereignty over a once unified Britain, and the hope of renewal. This broad motif would suffice for many national stories, but the surprising aspect in the British case is its ubiquity. Though the details are often different in different stories (sometimes greatly, sometimes slightly), the overall theme is constantly repeated. Even Gildas, our earliest British historian – if he is rightly described as a historian – viewed Britain as a discrete unit morally and historically and, though he admired the Romans, he consistently presented the Romans as 'them' and the Britons as 'us'. Gildas also couched Britain's history in terms of successive invasions, some advantageous (that of Rome), some disastrous (that of the Saxons). Gildas also looked to the Old Testament for narrative models. When the Israelites forgot God, He punished them by inflicting the loss of their homeland on them, using external foes as his instrument: this narrative model had the benefit both of a potentially wide application and of a significant authority. That this story, which also informed St Patrick's view of history, was formative in the evolution of the later British invasion narratives is not surprising. Thus, Gildas integrated the first of these two themes (sovereignty, loss of sovereignty) into his denunciation of contemporary Britain; the third, the notion of future recovery, is inherent at least putatively in his comparison of the British with the Israelites.

Gildas, therefore, can be seen to lie at the beginning of a long and thematically consistent tradition of medieval Welsh history and pseudo-history. *Historia Brittonum* provided an overall chronological framework as well as mentioning briefly several episodes that we find developed at greater length elsewhere. Geoffrey of Monmouth, with his enthusiastic embracing of *Historia Brittonum*'s outline and inherent themes, if not always its content, crowned this tradition and bestowed it on the Norman and, by extension, the European world. Geoffrey, moreover, unlike Gerald of Wales, endorsed the promise that the Britons (the Welsh and Bretons combined) would once more rule the whole of Britain. Gerald, while he predicted continued Welsh resistance to the 'English' – due in part to the memory of 'not only of their Trojan descent but also of the majesty of the kings of Britain, a kingdom which was so great and so enduring' (*Descriptio Kambriae*, Bk ii.10) – specifically limited this future sovereign territory to Wales rather than having it encompass the whole of Britain. While this was certainly a more realistic vision, it lacked the majesty of that of Welsh tradition and that of Geoffrey's *Historia*.

One of the most important stories in *Historia Brittonum* is that of the two contending dragons, which we can trace through both the British Latin and the Welsh traditions as a motif of sovereignty. This story begins with Vortigern (in Welsh, Gwrtheyrn), who appears by name first in Bede's *Ecclesiastical History*, and who is probably hinted at in Gildas's earlier account as the *superbus tyrannus* (perhaps a translation of the name Vortigern, which means 'over-lord') who, with his council, invites the first Saxon settlement as mercenaries. In his first appearance in *Historia Brittonum* (ch. 31), Vortigern is the ruler of Britain at the time of raids from the Picts and the Irish. Under pressure from these (as in Gildas's *De Excidio Britanniae*) and, less predictably, fearing a Roman invasion, Vortigern welcomes (and presumably has been instrumental in inviting) the three 'keels' of Saxons. The next time we see him (ch. 37), he grants the Saxons more land in exchange for the daughter of Hengest, one of their leaders, and invites more Saxons (ch. 38). After St Germanus and the entire British council condemn him (ch. 39), he and his magi decide to build a great fortress against the Saxons who, it is prophesied, will turn against him.

Vortigern and his magi set to building the fortress in Snowdonia, but their work each day disappears each night. Vortigern is ordered to find a magical child to sacrifice in order to put a stop to this, but the boy, once discovered, has his own advice (ch. 42). The boy relates that under the foundations is a lake, in which are two vessels, and between them a cloth. In the cloth (the hollow vessels, which, it is implied, contain something, are apparently superfluous) are two worms (*vermes*), one white and one red. Once the cloth is opened, the worms begin to fight each other; three times the white one almost pushes the red one to the edge of the cloth, but finally the red one drives the white off the cloth entirely. They both vanish beyond the lake. The magical boy explains that the cloth is Vortigern's kingdom and the lake is the world. The red worm is Vortigern's dragon (*draco*); the white is that of the invaders. 'Later', says the boy, 'our people will arise and will valiantly throw the English people across the sea'. The boy's name is revealed to be Ambrosius or Emrys, of a Roman consular family. He is given the site of the fortress to rule; the implication is that this is Dinas Emrys, an Iron Age hill fort in Gwynedd.

These dragons appeared in other texts, clearly connected with this story, although not always the same in their details. Moreover, the fact that vernacular Welsh tradition in its written form postdates Geoffrey's text means that the surviving versions are entangled with Geoffrey's own version, even those that may have originally ante-dated it. This is certainly the case with the tale *Cyfranc Lludd a Llefelys*. The tale relates how Llefelys, with his brother Lludd's permission, wooed and married the heiress to the French kingdom, and lived happily ever after. Then the story abruptly skips to relating three plagues (*gormesoedd*) that afflicted Britain: the first was the magical Coranieid, the second was an annual scream that left everything barren and the third was a giant who ate everyone's food. The second plague is of greatest interest, being revealed as the noise made by a dragon fighting a foreign dragon. Llefelys instructed Lludd to find these dragons in the exact centre of Britain (note that this relates to the whole of the island of Britain) by stratagems that partially resemble the instructions given by Ambrosius to Vortigern in *Historia Brittonum* as regards the uncovering of his dragons. Once he found the dragons, Lludd was told to bury them in a stone coffer. As long as they are concealed, the tale states, Britain will be safe from any plague. Lludd then concealed the dragons in Dinas Emrys (which is where the *Historia Brittonum* implies that they are buried), put a stop to all the plagues and lived in peace thereafter. This is clearly intended as an account of how Vortigern's dragons were put where he found them, although its implication that their uncovering put an end to any protection is absent from *Historia Brittonum*. In this the dragons of *Cyfranc Lludd a Llefelys* resemble Brân's head, the burial of which at the end of *Branwen* (the Second Branch of the Mabinogi) is described as one of the 'Three Happy Concealments' and whose uncovering (which is described in *Manawydan*, the Third Branch of the Mabinogi) is described as one of the 'Three Unhappy Disclosures'.

These statements in *Branwen* and *Manawydan* refer to a collection of references to notable events and characters, in groups of three as a mnemonic device, known as *Trioedd Ynys Prydein* ('Triads of the Island of Britain'). The triads, thought to have been put together around the twelfth century, group their items under titles which for the most part specify three notable things in *Ynys Prydein*, 'the Island of Britain'. Hence they shared with the Latin histories and the Welsh prose tales a symbolic belief that the island of Britain was or ought to have been a unified whole – some of the later triads replaced *Ynys Prydein* with *Llys Arthur*, 'Arthur's court', a 'de-nationalizing' process also seen in some Arthurian romances. One triad, 'Three Concealments and Three Disclosures of the Island of Britain' (no. 37 by the editor's numbering), is clearly that referred to in *Branwen*: one of its items is the concealment of the head of Brân and another is the dragons buried by Lludd son of Beli in Dinas Emrys in Eryri (Snowdonia), a relatively cryptic account of the matter of the *Cyfranc*. The triad, in contrast to *Historia Brittonum* and Geoffrey's *Historia* but in common with the *Cyfranc*, presented the burial of the dragons as one of three talismanic protective concealments whose effectiveness ended with their disclosure – that the other two involved human burial might suggest that the dragons supplanted an earlier notice of human burial. *Historia Brittonum* and *Historia Regum Britanniae*, however, presented explicitly symbolic dragons who enacted a long-term struggle not affected by its concealment or disclosure.

Cyfranc Lludd a Llefelys, unlike *Branwen* and *Manawydan*, does not directly cite any triads. The tale itself, however, is essentially an extended triad and clearly is closely related to another triad, 'Three Oppressions [*gormesoedd*] that came to this Island, and not one of them went back' (no. 36). In this triad, the three *gormesoedd* are the Coraniaid, from Arabia, the Gwyddyl Ffichti, that is the Picts, and the Saxons. It is not at all clear who the Coraniaid were intended to be, but it is possible that they were mistaken for the *Cesaryeit*, 'men of Caesar', as found in another triad, 'Three Levies that departed from this Island, and not one of them came back' (no. 35). 'The Three Oppressions', then, probably concerned historical or pseudo-historical invasions. While it is reasonable to assume that the *Cyfranc* originated in something similar, its import is different: the pseudo-historical events are instead folklorish fairy tales. While the Coraniaid appear in the *Cyfranc*, the Gwyddyl Ffichti appear to have been replaced with a giant and a battle between the Saxons and Britons, the third *gormes* in the triad, is only indirectly implied by the far less specific dragons of the *Cyfranc*. However, the dragons are not entirely obscure: according to the *Cyfranc*, the one dragon was fighting 'a dragon of a foreign people' ('dreic estrawn genedyl'), which can easily be connected with the Saxons who were clearly Britain's main foreign invader as far as the medieval Welsh tradition was concerned. Even poems that complained about Norman foes often reverted to describing them in terms of the various Anglo-Saxon peoples.

Although Geoffrey used the story of the dragons' disclosure mostly as it occurs in *Historia Brittonum* (albeit with at least one significant change, the replacement of Ambrosius with Merlin, discussed below in chapter 8), he did not include anything resembling the story of the concealment of the dragons. He did include a character whose name (Lud) and family relations were strikingly similar to Lludd. This suggests that he did know the story or something like it, particularly since Lludd was almost entirely unknown in surviving Welsh tradition apart from the *Cyfranc*; Llefelys, whom Geoffrey did not include, is almost completely obscure. Lludd and Llefelys are described in the *Cyfranc* as sons of Beli Mawr, himself very well attested and indeed an immensely important ancestor figure for the main medieval Welsh kingdoms as is clear from the genealogical material. Beli Mawr appears in the *Historia Brittonum*, in the tale *Breudwyt Maxen Wledic* (discussed below in chapter 5) and elsewhere as the British ruler in charge when the Romans conquered it and his son, Caswallon, is described in 'Three Levies that departed from this Island, and not one of them came back' (no. 35) as the one who pursued the men of Caesar to the continent, although it is not clear whether or not this was seen as a good thing, given the title of the triad. Caswallon also has a considerable profile elsewhere in medieval Welsh tradition as one who presided over Britain at the time of the Roman invasion, like his father. He probably harks back to the real Cassivellaunus, the leader of the British when Caesar invaded, according to Caesar's *De Bello Gallico* (Bk v.11–12). This is probably also Geoffrey's main source for his Cassibellaunus brother of Lud, whom he places in this same position. The question, then, is to what extent, if any, our Welsh characters, Beli, Lludd and Caswallon, owe their reputations to Geoffrey or what was Geoffrey's debt to pre-existing material.

Geoffrey, however, called Lud's father, who was clearly based on Beli Mawr, Heli, having used the name Beli elsewhere. Geoffrey named Heli's three sons as Lud, Cassibellaunus and Nennius (Bk iii.20) and said that they lived on the eve of the first Roman invasion. According to Geoffrey, considerable building works were carried out in Lud's reign. The only remarkable element thus far was the inclusion of Lud, given the apparent obscurity of the Welsh Lludd. But the point of this part of Geoffrey's story, as is very often the case with Geoffrey, is the explanation of a place-name, in this case Ludgate, where he is buried (Geoffrey scrupulously gave its British equivalent Porthlud). Thus we can explain Geoffrey's Lud with no reference to the material contained within *Cyfranc Lludd a Llefelys*, although it would be a coincidence, then, that Geoffrey associated Lud with his father Beli, here Heli. Heli's other son, Cassibellaunus, was clearly Caesar's Cassivellaunus, Welsh Caswallon. Caswallon's associations with Beli and with the Roman invasion pre-date Geoffrey, according to the evidence of the genealogical material in Oxford, Jesus College MS 20 (the manuscript dates from the fourteenth century but the material is considerably earlier). The quantity of similar material in Welsh tradition elsewhere, albeit in its current form post-dating Geoffrey,

35

strongly suggests that here Geoffrey was following, not creating, these relationships.

However, the fact that vernacular Welsh tradition post-dates Geoffrey in its written form means that the surviving versions are entangled with Geoffrey's own version. The textual history of *Cyfranc Lludd a Llefelys* exemplifies this fact and the difficulties it throws up for scholars. The tale is unique among the medieval Welsh prose tales making up the Mabinogion collection in existing outside its two main manuscript collections (the White Book of Rhydderch and the Red Book of Hergest); it was also inserted into most of the Welsh translations of Geoffrey's *Historia Regum Britanniae*, being placed after Geoffrey's account of the founding of London by Lud, with Geoffrey's Heli corrected to Beli and Cassibellaunus rendered as Caswallon. The *Cyfranc*, as found in these Welsh translations, visibly differs in its lack of descriptive flourishes from the other tales of the Mabinogion collection and indeed from the *Cyfranc* found in its Mabinogion context – this strongly suggests that there was a considerable difference in stylistic convention in terms of storytelling for different purposes. Otherwise the Mabinogion version is basically the same as the version found in the translations, retaining its setting as described by Geoffrey and stating that Lludd built Caer Lludd, London, in circumstances similar to those given by Geoffrey. It also shows Geoffrey's influence in listing Beli's three sons as Geoffrey lists them, but then says 'according to the story' ('herwyd y kyuar-wydyt') there was a fourth son, Llefelys. Elsewhere, if medieval Welsh tradition gives a number for the sons, the number is seven. Geoffrey's influence on this tale, however, is limited to this intro-ductory setting: it is not at all in evidence in the main content of the tale.

Assuming that Geoffrey knew the story of the *Cyfranc*, which is implied although not confirmed by the names of Lud's relations, Heli and Cassibellaunus, we can infer that although Geoffrey changed the details of this story entirely, he retained the identity of Beli and his family as a link between Rome and Britain. But Geoffrey used the name Beli or Belinus elsewhere, for a character whose activities, entirely invented by Geoffrey, represent not conquest of Britain by Rome but conquest of Rome by Britain. Geoffrey in fact used the name Belinus three times, twice for very minor characters (once for Cassibellaunus's commander-in-chief at the time of the Roman invasion of Britain (Bk iv.3); once in a list of ancestors of Caduanus, the king of the Venedoti who becomes ruler of Britain in the post-Arthurian period (Bk xii.6). In the third case, Geoffrey gave the name to a very important character, one who does the opposite of what Beli Mawr usually is presented as doing in medieval Welsh tradition: Geoffrey's Belinus son of Dunuallo, rather than presiding over the loss of Britain to the Romans (as Beli Mawr seemed to do), conquered large areas of Europe. Most impressively, he and his brother sacked Rome itself in the period before the Romans invaded Britain. Like Lud, Belinus gave his name to one of London's gates, in this case Billingsgate, *Belinesgata*. It seems entirely possible that Geoffrey derived the name for this character as a back-formation from Billingsgate, although surely the fact of Belinus's accomplishments presenting an inversion of those of Beli Mawr is more than a coincidence. Geoffrey's Belinus exemplifies the fact that the relationship between Britain and Rome was crucial to understanding British history, a theme shared by medieval Welsh historiographical tradition. But Geoffrey went further than this tradition by presenting it explicitly as having been forged, along with most of Britain's greatest achievements, in the period before the Roman invasion of Britain and thus as a British, rather than a Roman, accomplishment.

5

Britain and Rome

In continuing a historical tradition in which Rome and the Anglo-Saxons featured as invaders, Geoffrey saw the main agent of the loss of British sovereignty as the Anglo-Saxon invasion; this is clear from the story of the dragons. In this, Geoffrey was in agreement with Gildas and with *Historia Brittonum*, both of whom implied that Rome was the first, and in many ways the most profoundly affecting, invader: this was not necessarily, for either text, a bad thing. Moreover, through the character of Brutus, Britain's Trojan founder according to *Historia Brittonum* and Geoffrey's *Historia Regum Britanniae*, Britain could be seen to have been in a sense 'Roman' from the beginning. Medieval Welsh pseudo-historical writing developed this notion through figures, whether historical, legendary or in between, such as Magnus Maximus, the Maxen of Welsh tradition, who is discussed in detail in chapter 6 below. As we will see, their relevance to, and at times origins in, Britain were highlighted or even invented, thus allowing British dynasties to trace their origins to rulers of the Roman empire. Through such figures the relationship between Britain and Rome would not be one solely, or even chiefly, of conquest of the former by the latter. Indeed, in having essentially British figures go, or return, to Rome to rule, thus reversing the direction of conquest, Britain could claim rulership of Rome and through her the known world. Geoffrey's writings developed this theme with visible enthusiasm, and it is one of the hallmarks of his great debt to medieval Welsh pseudo-historical tradition. But he went further than Welsh tradition in giving Britain a significant pre-Roman history, something that no other Welsh text had done to any extent.

For Gildas, history essentially began with the Romans. Gildas presented Roman Britain as a pleasant and well-equipped place (including sturdily built cities and buildings). He had little to say about her people before the time of the Romans, except that she was 'full of tyrants' (ch. 4.4). *Historia Brittonum* took a different tack entirely, connecting the very foundation of Britain, indirectly, with Rome. It stated that Britain took its name from 'one Brutus, a Roman consul' (ch. 7). As in the case of the origins of the Irish, it gave two alternative explanations for Britain's origins: the first, ascribed to the 'Annals of the Romans', related how Brutus or Britto, the grandson of the Trojan hero Aeneas (himself the founder of Rome, according to Virgil's *Aeneid*), was prophesied as 'the child of death', who would 'kill his father and mother and become hateful to all men' (ch. 10). Having accidentally killed his father, Brutus was driven from Italy and eventually wandered to Gaul, where he founded Tours, before coming to Britain to be its founder and eponym. The name Brutus was probably derived from St Jerome's translations of Eusebius's *Chronicon*: according to Eusebius, a Brutus, the Roman consul Decimus Junius Brutus Callaicus, conquered Spain in 142 BC. *Historia Brittonum* appears to have added Britain to Brutus's conquests and put the tale into a Trojan context. Brutus's epithet, 'hateful', may well derive from Isidore of Seville's *Etymologies* (early seventh century), which suggested that the British were so called because they were 'brutes' (Bk ix.2). The name Brutus also evokes the legendary co-founder of the Roman republic, Lucius Junius Brutus, best known from Livy's *Ab urbe condita*.

The second explanation given in *Historia Brittonum* was perhaps originally attached to a separate figure, Britto or Britus, eponym of the Brittones. It traced two slightly different genealogies for Britto (chs 17 and 18). The first was derived from an early medieval text (sixth century?) examining the supposed genealogical relations between the various Roman and post-Roman barbarian ethnic groups, known as the 'fränkische Völkertafel' or 'Frankish Table of Nations'. It had its basis in Tacitus's account of the Germans as divided into three peoples, representing descent from the three sons of the god Mannus: the Ingaevones (or Ingvaeones), the

Herminones and the Istaevones (*Germania*, Bk i.2). Most versions of the medieval text enumerated the peoples descended from one of the three brothers, Istio, as the Romans (*Romanos*), Britons (*Brittones* or *Brictones*), Franks (*Francus* or *Francos*) and Alemanni (*Alamannus* or *Alamannos*). The version in *Historia Brittonum* rendered the father as Hessitio and the sons as Francus, Romanus, Britto and Albanus who were the ancestors of the *Franci*, *Latini*, *Albani* and *Britti*. Thus, through Britto the Britons were linked not only to the Romans but to founding ancestors of several other post-Roman European peoples. The version found in *Historia Brittonum* is unique in providing a greatly expanded context for this text, drawing in not only the Trojans but also the sons of Noah. Its resemblance to later constructions found in the Irish material, in particular in *Lebor Gabála Érenn*, suggests that some of its particularities might derive from a particular insular source common to both.

The *Aeneid*'s account of the Trojan diaspora provided a convenient slot in which the historians of post-Roman kingdoms could situate their origins – origins that must have been particularly attractive in their proximity and indeed anteriority to the origins of Rome itself. The notion of Trojan ancestry is found in medieval histories of Franks (notably the Chronicle of Fredegar), Scandinavians (Snorri Sturluson's *Prose Edda*) and Normans (Dudo of Saint-Quentin's *Gesta Normannorum* and William of Jumièges's *Gesta Normannorum Ducum*). Nor were such speculations confined to post-Roman peoples: according to classical writers such as Lucan and Ammianus Marcellinus, the Gauls, in particular the Aedui or Arverni (or both), claimed to be of Trojan descent. Julius Caesar also described the Aedui as 'brothers and kinsmen' in *De Bello Gallico* (Bk i.33). *Historia Brittonum* is unique, however, in the genealogical complexity of the claim to Trojan ancestry. No other versions of the Frankish Table locate their Old Testament-derived schemes within a Trojan context. We may recall, as well, that the tales of Irish origins found in *Historia Brittonum* and later *Lebor Gabála Érenn* eschewed the Trojan context entirely, and concentrated on a wandering ancestor connected to a Scythian nobleman who lived at the time of the Exodus.

Despite figuring so prominently in *Historia Brittonum*, Brutus did not make much of an impression on Welsh tradition, if the genealogical material pre-dating Geoffrey is anything to go by. We should perhaps note that the eponymous ancestor of the text *Enweu Ynys Brydein*, 'The Names of the Island of Britain' (twelfth century but probably incorporating older material), is named Prydein son Aedd. Prydein, the tract says, gave Britain its name, having conquered it in the last of a series of invasions, which is very reminiscent of the *Lebor Gabála Érenn*. Prydein also appears in several genealogies, although not as a founding figure, in post-Geoffrey Welsh texts. *Historia Brittonum* does not mention him at all, and he is notably absent from Geoffrey's *Historia Regum Britanniae*.

Geoffrey, as was his habit, retained the bare outlines sketched in *Historia Brittonum*'s first explanation of Britain's origins, but greatly expanded them (he ignored the second entirely). He presented Brutus as Aeneas's great-grandson (*Historia Brittonum* had Brutus either as Aeneas's grandson (ch. 10) or his great-great-grandson (ch. 18)), although his account of the family relationships was not entirely consistent. Geoffrey built on the description of the Trojan diaspora in the *Aeneid* and extended it to northern Europe, falsely claiming Homer as a source for Brutus's foundation of Tours (Bk i.14). Like Aeneas, Brutus was informed of his destiny in founding an empire through a prophecy: Diana appeared to Brutus in a vision and informed him that he was to found 'a new Troy' to which the entire world would be subject (Bk i.11). Brutus and his companions met up with a second set of Trojans (descendants of Antenor) led by Corineus, the future founder of Cornwall (Bk i.12), whose name, doubtlessly taken from the *Aeneid*, must have resonated with Geoffrey in his search for eponymous ancestors. Through Corineus, Cornwall had a different, although equal, Trojan origin and a different lineage of rulers, one that supplied deficiencies in the main British line at crucial vacancies. According to Geoffrey, Brutus came to what was then called Albion and found it empty except for a few giants. He and his companion set to inhabiting and naming this empty land: Britain was derived from Brutus, Cornwall from Corineus. Brutus's sons Locrinus, Kamber and Albanactus gave their names to England ('Loegria', *Lloegr* in Welsh), Wales ('Kambria', a Latinization of the Welsh word for Wales and the Welsh, *Cymry*) and Scotland ('Albania', 'Scotland in our language –

lingua nostra'; Bk ii.1). These three sons were entirely Geoffrey's invention. On the Thames, Brutus built Trinovantum, a British name that Geoffrey presumably knew from *Historia Brittonum*, in which it was the site of Julius Caesar's decisive victory over the British (ch. 20) – this probably had its ultimate origin in Julius Caesar's account of the *Trinovantes* who lived near Cassivellaunus's capital town in *De Bello Gallico* (Bk v.20–2). According to Geoffrey, Trinovantum was derived from Troia Nova, 'New Troy', and became Trinovantum 'through corruption' ('per corruptionem', Bk i.17).

At this point, somewhat uncharacteristically, Geoffrey paused to dwell on the future of the site: looking forward he noted that at the time of the Roman invasion of Britain, Lud, who fought against Julius Caesar, changed the name to Kaerlud, 'Lud's city', an act that sparked dissension between him and his brother Nennius, 'who was indignant that Lud wished to suppress the name of Troy in the realm'. Geoffrey went on to argue that since Gildas 'the historian' had dealt with this quarrel at length, he would not bother, citing his insufficiency of style compared with that of Gildas. Gildas says nothing of the quarrel.

It is characteristic of Geoffrey's approach that his account of Britain's earliest days is not straightforward in presenting original 'Trojan' (Latin?) origins as overlaid, later, by British ones. Although in the case of Trinovantum he seemed to be suggesting that an original Latin name (Troia Nova) was corrupted into a British form (Trinovantum), the process was not straightforward: a politically motivated change to another British form, Kaerlud, then led to another corruption, Kaerlundein. Even this was not the final form: as 'time passed and languages changed', it became Lundene and then 'when foreigners landed and conquered the country' a further change rendered it Lundres (Bk iii.20), an unusually clear reference to the Normans. At least in this case we can trace a series of changes with a visible and reasonable chronology. Elsewhere, Geoffrey had the process moving in the opposite direction, from British to Latin. He explicitly commented that the River Severn, Sabrina in Latin, was a corruption of an original British name, Habren (in modern Welsh the river's name is Hafren). He strengthened the point by relating a story (invented by him) of the doomed British princess Habren (Bk ii.5).

Clearly, Geoffrey was not concerned with extinguishing a pre-Trojan history in Britain: it helped that through the device of Brutus's 'Trojan' language, which was clearly 'British' and classical – 'Crooked Greek', discussed in chapter 9 – Geoffrey could have it both ways (Bk i.16). Geoffrey's refusal to produce a coherent sequential process from Trojan to British or British to Trojan reflects the fact that, for him, the Trojans are seen amongst a number of early peoples in a broad rather than narrow sequence of British history. In this he can be seen as diverging from an 'invasion and replacement' vision of the peopling of Britain.

Neither Gildas, *Historia Brittonum* nor any other medieval Welsh text had anything of substance to say about events in Britain before the invasion of Rome. Geoffrey, however, attributed the major events of building and culture to the pre-Roman, albeit of shared Trojan/Roman descent, Britons. Such famous Roman achievements as Caerleon and Bath became in Geoffrey's scheme works of the pre-Roman occupants. The only significant exception to this was Stonehenge, which according to Geoffrey was built by Merlin during the post-Roman period. Even the Anglo-Saxon laws known to the Normans from Alfred the Great and others as 'Mercian' were British and pre-Roman British at that, a production of Queen Marcia, their misattribution a result of Alfred's mistake in translating their title as *Merchenelage* (Bk iii.13). Surely this was a bold claim, even for Geoffrey? Geoffrey was clearly determined to situate within this Trojan, pre-Roman period the establishment of every aspect of a civilized society. This goes beyond merely removing the stigma of the historical Roman conquest of AD 43: pre-Roman Britain was a rival as well as a cousin to Rome; Brutus, while akin to the Trojans who would go on to found Rome, made Britain a new Troy, rivalling Virgil's Rome to an extent that was more than a simple 'flag of convenience' borrowing classical glory. Geoffrey was, more than anything else, determined to stress Britain's unimpeachable position in the world of antiquity.

At this point we confront the scale of Geoffrey's creation. Geoffrey named some sixty-five British kings and three queens (not counting unsuccessful usurpers) as reigning after Brutus and before Cassibellaunus, the king at the time of the invasion of Britain by Julius Caesar. The sheer number of them was to cause concern to the twelfth-century Norman historian Robert of Torigni when he contemplated inserting them into the usual lists of notable events in history as found in the Eusebian/Hieronymian calculations described above. Most of their reigns were described briefly, if at all, but several were given significantly more attention. The first to be described at length was Leir, whose story Geoffrey seemed to have invented entirely (but which has persisted long after Geoffrey), with its suggestive parallels between the positions of Cordeilla and Geoffrey's contemporary, Matilda. The second was Dunuallo Molmutius, discussed above with reference to the Molmutine laws. His activities showed that the Britons were able to legislate and engage in significant public works well before the Roman invasion. The third British ruler whose career was discussed at length was Belinus (who is sometimes referred to as Beli in some manuscripts), Dunuallo's son, whose name Geoffrey seemed to have adopted from the entirely different, and by no means insignificant, figure, Beli Mawr. Belinus went beyond his father's achievements: he ruled, at least for a time, Rome itself. Initially, Belinus, the older and rightful king of Britain was at war with his brother Brennius, who had ambitions beyond his younger son's portion of northern Britain. Brennius allied himself with the Norwegians and the Danes, in an encapsulation of Northumbrian history. After Belinus defeated Brennius they made peace and joined forces to conquer Rome. Geoffrey modelled this, not surprisingly, on the sack of Rome by the Gauls in the late fourth century BC, which various classical and medieval sources attributed to Brennus, the leader of the Gaulish Senonians (Geoffrey even gave Brennius a Gaulish context by having him marry into the ruling house of the Allobroges, Bk iii.6). Brennius stayed behind to rule Rome, 'where he subjected the people to unparalleled oppression' (Bk iii.10) – presumably this is a criticism – and Belinus returned to rule Britain, presiding over a period of prosperity that Geoffrey, somewhat ominously, stated would never be equalled (Bk iii.10). As Geoffrey did not describe Brennius's ultimate fate, or say who his successor was, it would seem that there was no sequel to the British rule of Rome for some generations. After Belinus's death, Geoffrey noted the rules of some forty further kings until he came to the invasion by Rome at the time of King Heli and his sons.

Geoffrey shared the ambivalence of his sources as regards the Roman invasion of Britain. While it is abundantly clear that Gildas admired the Romans and considered Britain's period under Roman rule to have been its golden age, he presented the initial Roman invasion of Britain as that of a foreign, relatively oppressive force. Unlike other peoples conquered by the Romans, Gildas stated that the British were not subdued by war but by 'mere threats and legal penalties' (ch. 5.2). It is difficult to tell if this was a good or bad thing as Gildas saw it, but his subsequent narration reveals that it was in fact a sign of British cowardice. Roman governors were slain by the 'treacherous' British, necessitating the return of Roman troops who proved again the uselessness of the British in war and established a less benign, more militaristic rule. *Historia Brittonum* related that the Romans, having conquered the entire world (this is reminiscent of Gildas's account), sent to Britain asking for hostage and tax (ch. 19). The author's view is somewhat ambiguous: the British were 'arrogant and turbulent' for refusing this request and Julius Caesar's anger (justified?) caused him to invade. It is striking, however, that the text states 'on account of [the departure of the Romans] Britain had been occupied by foreigners (*occupata est ab extraneis gentibus*) and her citizens expelled until God shall give them help' (ch. 27): clearly, the Romans, whatever else they were, were not 'foreigners'. One is reminded here of Geoffrey's justification of Arthur's refusal of the same demand from Rome at the height of his career (Bk ix.6), a justification that Arthur, the conqueror, unconvincingly and self-servingly based on the idea that conquest did not legitimate gains. Gildas, the author of *Historia Brittonum* and Geoffrey are similar in considering the Roman invasion of Britain as both legitimate and illegitimate.

Geoffrey's account of Julius Caesar's invasion began with Caesar himself acknowledging the common Trojan descent of both Romans and Britons. As we have seen above, this could have been derived from Caesar's own writings, albeit indirectly. According to Geoffrey, Caesar expected that he would find the Britons to be degenerate and unsophisticated. He sent a message asking for tribute, which was angrily replied to by Cassibellaunus, who also cited their common Trojan ancestry and asserted their historical freedom from conquest (Bk iv.2). In contradiction to Gildas's account of the spineless British, Geoffrey's British were conquered imperfectly and with great difficulty. Claudius overcame the British leader Aruiragus (who was named as a British king in Juvenal's Fourth Satire, presumably Geoffrey's source) not by force but by asking for recognition of Rome's overlordship. Moreover, Claudius offered his daughter, Gewissa, in marriage to Aruiragus, linking their ruling houses. When Vespasian was sent by Claudius to force Aruiragus to re-submit to Rome, Aruiragus, having become powerful enough to disregard the Romans, the battle was inconclusive and Gewissa mediated a peaceful settlement. Their line of kings lasted for three more generations, with the final king, Lucius, a convert to Christianity, dying without an heir (Bk v.1) and ushering in an era of Roman and British claimants and usurpers which was notably brief (encompassing some ten rulers) compared with the era of the pre-Roman British kings (encompassing some sixty rulers).

Historia Brittonum listed several Roman emperors to come to Britain. The first was Julius Caesar; the second was Claudius. The third was Severus, who built a wall in the north – this clearly refers to Severus's refurbishment of Hadrian's wall. The fourth emperor was Carausius – a historically attested Roman naval commander who set himself up as emperor in Britain in the late third century, and whose rule was characterized by significant trappings of imperial legitimacy including his own coinage. The fifth was Constantine, described as the son of Constantine the Great in all but one manuscript, which has the reading we might expect, that is, 'father', given that these probably represent Constantius I and his son Constantine I. Having gained imperial power in the west and over-seen the defeat of Carausius, Constantius I died at Eburacum (York) in 306, at which point his son Constantine I ('The Great') was proclaimed emperor by their British troops. Both Constantine I and his mother Helena figured significantly in medieval views of

Britain's Roman history and are discussed below. The sixth was Maximus, that is Magnus Maximus, who is probably the most important figure in the medieval Welsh texts that concern themselves with Cambricizing Britain's Roman past. The seventh, Maximianus, is a doublet of the sixth (Maximus will be discussed below). The author of *Historia Brittonum* noted that his British sources only gave seven, but said that Roman sources named two more: another Severus (probably Severus II, whose position as emperor in the west Constantine I usurped). The ninth and last-named emperor was Constantius (Constantine III, d.411), the final commander to take Roman troops from Britain – it is striking, however, that in medieval Welsh tradition, Magnus Maximus's withdrawal of troops was made much of, whereas that of Constantine III, who presided over what was probably the final retreat on the eve of disaster for Roman Britain, was almost entirely unmentioned. It might be argued that Maximus, the more successful of the two, was a more attractive figure, although if we were looking for historical models of British-based pretenders to Roman imperial rule, surely the best candidate would be Carausius. Carausius, however, was unknown to medieval Welsh tradition outside *Historia Brittonum* until Geoffrey included him in his writings.

Carausius presents a relatively straightforward example of Geoffrey adapting a story, minimally, to suit his theme. Geoffrey took his account of Carausius (Bk v.3–4) mostly from Bede, but made several minor changes: he made Carausius British rather than merely located in Britain. He changed the dating of the episode, retaining not Bede's accurate chronology but *Historia Brittonum*'s muddled one and thus placing Carausius much earlier than he should be. Geoffrey also added a detail not found in other texts: he made Carausius responsible for settling the Picts in Scotland, providing them with an origin legend. A gloss in a mid-eleventh-century manuscript of *Historia Brittonum* (Cambridge, Corpus Christi College MS. 139) connected Carausius with the building of a wall (clearly the Antonine wall) on the river Carron in Stirlingshire on the borders of Pictland. This river, the gloss stated, took its name from him. Whether or not Geoffrey made a connection between Carausius and Scotland for the same reasons, or even based on this source, is an open question. Translations of Geoffrey's *Historia* into Welsh rendered the name as Carawn or Caron, a character who was ultimately turned into a saint and the supposed eponym of Tregaron, in Ceredigion. This place-name, however, was probably derived from a river name, as in Scotland. The entire process owed much to English antiquarians, and Geoffrey was clearly a significant linking element in the meeting of Welsh and English histories.

Some stories Geoffrey seems to have ignored, in particular those associated with the origins of the post-Roman Welsh kingdoms. The well-known character Cunedda, the ancestor figure of the medieval dynasty ruling Gwynedd, who was mentioned several times in *Historia Brittonum* (chs 14 and 62), became Cunedagius in Geoffrey's account, a minor ruler who usurped Cordeilla, although he did rule well for a number of years and founded a dynasty. Other ancestor figures gave their names to far less prominent characters in Geoffrey's *Historia*: Ceredig, the eponymous ancestor of Ceredigion mentioned in genealogies as well as in the lives of St Carantoc (*Vita I*, ch. 1, *Vita II*, chs 1–4), probably lay behind Geoffrey's Kareticus, who was Malgo's successor as king of Britain (Bk xi.8). Malgo himself bore the name of Gwynedd's most famous ruler, Maelgwn, and the connection between the two may reflect the fact that at some point Ceredig's story was attached to that of Cunedda, the reputed founder of Maelgwn's dynasty. Geoffrey treated both Malgo and Kareticus dismissively, Malgo as a good ruler but given to vice, and Kareticus as a bad ruler, whose weakness encouraged the Saxons. At least one Welsh founding figure, one who figured in the genealogies that Geoffrey certainly used, was entirely ignored: this is Brychan, the eponymous ancestor of Brycheiniog.

This perhaps underscores the point that Geoffrey's interest lay in Britain as opposed to Wales. When Geoffrey came to the end of his history, he noted that the people to whom he had mainly, although not exclusively, referred to as *Brittones* (he used *Gualiae* seven times) had, through their failings become known as *Gualenses*, 'Welsh', either from a ruler Gualo, from a Queen Galaes or from their decline. Geoffrey's dismissiveness about the term can be explained partly with reference to his repeated contention that the British settlement of Armorica left Britain populated by less noble remnants (Bks vi.2; vi.4; xii.5; xii.6). It can also be explained with reference to the term 'Welsh' itself, a pejorative originating in the Anglo-Saxon word *wealh*, originally meaning 'foreigner' but quickly coming to indicate a person of lower status and, often, a slave. Geoffrey was, apparently, consistent: the heroes of *Historia Regum Britanniae* were the ancient British; their heirs were the continental Bretons. However, Geoffrey's geographical and political landscape was extremely complicated. At its foundations, Britain was one political unit founded by Brutus, and Geoffrey repeatedly stressed this unity: Arthur, for example, 'should have been ruler of the entire island by lawful inheritance' (Bk ix.1); the British, and initially the Saxons, were criticized for not being willing to establish a single kingship (Bk xi.11); the Saxons' ultimate and in the context legitimate success was due to their willingness to submit to one king, Athelstan (Bk xii.19). Nevertheless, even as Brutus was creating Britain, there was also a smaller kingdom within the island: one region fell to the share of Corineus, and was called Cornwall (Bk i.16) – it retained a relatively autonomous identity throughout Geoffrey's tale. Moreover, later on Brutus's three sons, who did not figure in any texts before Geoffrey, divided the kingdom of Britain between them, with one, Kamber, taking the region 'now known as Wales (*Gualia*)'. Geoffrey explains that this region 'for a long time was named Kambria after him and for this reason the inhabitants still call themselves Cymry in British' ('gens patriae lingua Britannica sese Kambro appellat', Bk ii.1). The term Cambria, so familiar to us today, does not appear in any existing text that pre-dates Geoffrey, although its meaning was not invented by him. It is, as Geoffrey stated, a Latinization of the word for the Welsh in the Welsh language, *Cymry*, and while this coining is not unremarkable, the point is that Geoffrey seems to have been the one to have coined it. Indeed, Cambria failed to catch on as a term for Wales among other Anglo-Norman, Cambro-Norman and even Welsh writers; its only advocate, a very determined one, was Gerald of Wales, Giraldus Cambrensis, Geoffrey's often vehement critic in other matters. Most other Cambro-Latin writers and Welsh rulers continued to use some form of *Wallia* or *Wallenses*.

Thus, while at the end of *Historia Regum Britanniae* Geoffrey dismissed the Welsh as 'unworthy successors to the noble Britons' (Bk xii.20), at the very beginning of the text he made them into the Cambrians, a term that was ennobled by its associations with the ancient, heroic British. Geoffrey made no explicit connection between the two, and did not mention Kambria in his final account of the Welsh, so it is not clear how Geoffrey saw their relationship. Moreover, the political geography of Geoffrey's Britain is not consistent – although Britain was a whole kingdom yet divided, its four main component kingdoms fluctuated in their significance and even in their importance. At times, they were merely geographical designations (Bk iv.15); at times they were diocesan divisions (Bk iv.19). Geoffrey's account of Dunuallo Molmutius described how there was civil war between 'all the kings of Britain' who were five in number (Bk ii.17) – this seems to be Cornwall, Loegria, Kambria and Albania and presumably a fifth who was the legitimate ruler (these five kings also mirrored, in number, the five rulers criticized by Gildas). Dunuallo managed by conquest to control the entire island, and made himself a crown of gold to signify his unitary rule. In the very next section, however, Geoffrey described how Dunuallo's two sons, Belinus and Brennius, divided the kingdom between themselves according to 'Trojan' inheritance custom (specifically defended by Geoffrey), with the elder getting Loegria, Kambria, Cornwall and the crown, and the younger getting Northumbria, which included Scotland (Albania). This arrangement was peacefully observed for five years. Eventually it led to civil war, and the younger brother was disposed of – sent to rule Rome – so that the elder could once again rule an undivided kingdom (Bks iii.1–10). Geoffrey did not attribute the multiplicity of kings before Dunuallo specifically to customs of inheritance; the fact that the division between Dunuallo's sons did not immediately lead to war suggests that here, as well, division of the kingdom was not automatically catastrophic.

Other regional divisions were introduced so that Geoffrey could introduce new characters who, for one reason or another, should not be aligned with existing kingdoms. Octavius, Vortigern, Merlin and Cadualadrus's unnamed mother came from the otherwise obscure

Gewissei, who may well be intended as the people of Gwent, especially given Geoffrey's probable origins in Monmouth – certainly this is how Geoffrey's Welsh translators interpreted them. Geoffrey sometimes divided Wales into south and north, Demetia and Venedotia or Venedocia as Geoffrey termed them, using well-known terms of long standing based on Welsh names. Geoffrey used Demetia and Venedotia mainly as geographical designations, but ones with a very strong regional identity: Demetia had a 'metropolitan city' (*metropolis*) called Kaerusc, that is, Caerleon (Bk iii.10). Frequently, the peoples of these regions joined battle as distinct groups, as for example when the Demeti or Demetae and Venedoti, along with the Deiri and Albani (the latter one of Britain's main kingdoms, here listed with the regional ones) came to assist Asclepiodotus, Carausius's successor as king of Britain (Bk v.4). Surprisingly frequently, considering the importance of a unified rule of Britain to the overall trajectory of *Historia Regum Britanniae,* Geoffrey named rulers of these and, sometimes, other regions. We first meet them fighting the Romans under Cassibellaunus, where they were specifically subject to the main king of Britain: 'three sub-kings (*reges subditi*), Cridious of Albania, Gueithaet of Venedocia and Brithel of Demetia' (Bk iv.3). Merlin's mother was the daughter of the king (*rex*) of Demetia (Bk vi.17). Among the rulers present at Arthur's great court at Caerleon were Caduallo Lauhir, king of the Venedoti, and Stater, king of the Demetae – both are *rex* as well as one, Urien, to whom Arthur had returned 'ancestral rights' in making him king of Moray (Bks ix.9, 11). At the end of Arthur's great feast, the two kings of Demetia and Venedotia took their places by him, along with two others, kings of Albania and Cornwall (Bk ix.13). This represents a significant elevation in status for the two Welsh kingdoms which have apparently superseded Kambria, itself unmentioned. Loegria also has gone unmentioned. Geoffrey had clearly abandoned Kambria, its last appearance being an episode in which a comet appeared to Uther (Bk viii.15). Instead, especially after Arthur's court, Geoffrey named other individual kings (*reges*) of Demetia and Venedotia in passing (Bks xi.3, xii.1, xii.12).

Geoffrey also took liberties with the local and wider metropolitan controversies of his day. According to *Historia Regum*

Britanniae, Britain had three archbishoprics: one at London, one at York and one at Caerleon (Bk iv.19). According to Geoffrey's description of Arthur's grand court at Caerleon, Dubricius was archbishop of Caerleon and David, Arthur's uncle, was his successor in that post (Bk ix.15). Samson, we are told elsewhere, was archbishop of York (Bk viii.12). This confounds claims in Geoffrey's own time: the claim by Canterbury to primacy over Wales (as well as over York); the claim by St Davids to metropolitan status supported in part by the notion that Dubricius preceded David who was then succeeded by Samson, who then carried the pallium to Brittany, to Dol; claims by Llandaff to have authority over part of the diocese of St Davids; claims that Samson was not an archbishop in Britain, but only in Brittany and that Dubricius was an archbishop of Llandaff. The various arguments with respect to Welsh ecclesiastical organization were all abandoned in favour of Caerleon, surely a sign of Geoffrey's attitude of a pox on all their houses (except Caerleon).

Geoffrey's geographical perspectives support the argument that he came from south Wales, which featured far more profoundly, and with arguably greater local familiarity, in *Historia Regum Britanniae* than north Wales did. His relative lack of interest in northern British and southern Scottish history may not just have been the result of a lack of personal knowledge, however: it may help to locate him, and his sources, within the broader spectrum of medieval Welsh literary and historical tradition. The historians and pseudo-historians of Wales seem to have used a frame of reference slightly different from that of the court poets of the medieval Welsh princes. The latter mainly, although not exclusively, located the golden age of British heroism in northern Britain in the post-Roman period. They most often featured heroes known as *Gwŷr y Gogledd*, 'Men of the North', such as Urien and Owein. Geoffrey also included these characters in *Historia Regum Britanniae* and *Vita Merlini*, the latter far more than the former, which we will discuss below. In *Historia Regum Britanniae*, they were relatively minor characters mainly associated with Scotland, in which Geoffrey was clearly less interested. By contrast, the iconic heroes of historical or pseudo-historical prose were drawn predominantly from the

Roman period, not just from Britons but also from Romans themselves – this is true of *Historia Regum Britanniae* as well. Some of these Romans, in particular Magnus Maximus, or Maxen as he came to be known in Welsh tradition, were well known elsewhere in medieval Welsh literature and had become significantly 'Cambricized' independently of Geoffrey. Their importance in Welsh tradition mirrored their position in Geoffrey's scheme of British history. It is difficult to say whether the prominence of Magnus Maximus in medieval Welsh historiographical tradition was in fact due to Geoffrey, or if Geoffrey's view of him was as a result of existing Welsh tradition – arguments about whether Geoffrey lay at the beginning of or in the middle of a process of literary embellishment are notoriously difficult. However, we might contrast Magnus Maximus's fortunes to the continuing obscurity, as far as the Welsh were concerned, of a character whom we are quite certain was one of Geoffrey's inventions and one of his more significant characters, Belinus son of Dunuallo. Belinus's accomplishments, unequalled by any British leader including Arthur, seemed not to have been sufficient to insert him into medieval Welsh tradition. As regards Carausius, who was also extremely important in Geoffrey's scheme of Romano-British history, he was known among the Welsh but was much better known among the English. Geoffrey's influence in Wales, where it exceeded traditional material entirely, had its limits.

Geoffrey's detail can sometimes seem overwhelming, sometimes contradictory, and its context often obscure. Sometimes the apparent contradiction is due to his use of different sources; in most cases we see the thrust of his narrative when we consider it in a longer, not an immediate context. Geoffrey's theme is Britain, across the reign of dozens of kings. Inconsistency of foreground detail was of little moment.

6

Magnus Maximus and the Colonization of Brittany

Apart from Arthur, Magnus Maximus is probably the most prominent ruler depicted in medieval Welsh tradition. The transformation of the usurping Roman imperial pretender of history, Magnus Maximus, into the important hero and ancestor figure of Welsh genealogy, Macsen Wledig, presents a good example of the vast gap between historical events and how they might be portrayed in later medieval sources. Geoffrey contributed to this process, but in doing so he did not depart in any significant way from Maxen's securely established historiographical role. Maxen's relative coherence as a character was probably due to the fact that his career exemplified an extremely important aspect of medieval Welsh historical tradition that connected Britain and Rome, not only by making Britain Roman, but also by making the Roman empire British. Magnus Maximus not only exemplified these Roman and British connections, he stood at the end of them, an end that had catastrophic implications as it led to the Anglo-Saxon invasions that finally deprived the British of their sovereignty. Another crucial event linked to his reign, one connected with the departure of the Roman troops, was the foundation of Brittany. These pivotal events found their fullest exploration in Geoffrey's *Historia* – indeed they encapsulate its main themes. But Geoffrey's role was to elaborate rather than to invent the implications of this character's role in British history.

Magnus Maximus was the Spanish commander of the Roman army in Britain whose troops proclaimed him emperor in 383. He then took his troops to the continent and there won command over part of the western Roman empire for five years, being recognized as emperor of Gaul, Britain and Spain by Theodosius the Great, emperor in the eastern Roman empire. In 388, not content with his partial *imperium*, he invaded Rome but was killed by Theodosius's troops. He was named by Gildas as one of those who betrayed Britain by weakening Rome's power there, leaving her open to raids by barbarians (*De Excidio Britanniae*, chs 13–14). As noted above, he also appeared in *Historia Brittonum* as both Maximus, the sixth Roman emperor to come to Britain, and as Maximianus, the seventh. Maximus is clearly Magnus Maximus: *Historia Brittonum* said he spoke with St Martin (ch. 26) and we know this to be true of Magnus Maximus, as attested by St Martin's biographer Sulpicius Severus. *Historia Brittonum* then gave as the seventh emperor Maximianus, but some manuscripts reflected the confusion by saying that Maximianus was called Maximus (ch. 27). According to *Historia Brittonum*, Maximianus withdrew his troops from Britain, killed Gratian (described as 'king of the Romans'), held all of Europe and settled his soldiers on the continent as the first Armorican British. *Historia Brittonum*, as quoted in the previous chapter, stated unequivocally that the departure of these troops represented a turning point after which Britain was overrun by 'foreigners'. Thus, *Historia Brittonum* combined Gildas's apparently reasonable but historically untrue contention that Maximus's withdrawal of Roman troops fatally weakened Britain, leaving her open to invasion, with a different assertion, apparently reasonable but historically untrue, that Maximus's troops were responsible for the British settlement of what became Brittany. The connection of these two events is implicit in every medieval text from Wales and Brittany touching on this subject matter – they are entirely consistent in this sense, whatever the difference in their details.

Characteristically, *Historia Brittonum* then gave 'a second report of the tyrant Maximianus' (ch. 29). This account sketched events in the fourth century, presumably drawing upon written Roman sources, mentioned St Martin again and switched to the form 'Maximus' part way through. A further complicating factor in terms of the names used is that one of the two emperors against whom Carausius revolted was named Maximian (d.310; the other was Diocletian) and Maximian's son Maxentius (who was half-brother to Constantius I's second wife Theodora), who was condemned as a usurper but defeated by Constantine in 312. It would seem that although Maxentius had no hint of any British connection, he was confused with Maximus, who himself had a doublet, perhaps because of Constantine's own strong British connections (also in the process of elaboration). The names for the Romano-British emperor in the Welsh sources probably reflect this confusion: the earliest Latin sources, Gildas and *Historia Brittonum*, used Maximus or Maximianus; the earliest Welsh sources, the Harleian genealogies, used Maxim, which is Maximus without the Latin suffix. Welsh sources of the twelfth century and later regularly used the form Maxen, derived from Maxentius, instead of Maxim.

Of the three Roman emperors with British connections named in *Historia Brittonum* – Carausius, Magnus Maximus and Constantine – Maximus, as Maxim or Maxen, was seized upon as the embodiment of 'British' rulers of Rome. In this role he appeared in the medieval Welsh genealogical material as the founding figure of a number of post-Roman Welsh kingdoms, bridging the gap between the departure of Rome and the legendary origins of independent post-Roman British kingdoms, bestowing legitimacy and *Romanitas* upon these – 'a pleasing irony, in view of his actual history as a usurper', in the words of David Dumville. Our earliest evidence of this appeared in our earliest surviving Welsh genealogy, on the Pillar of Eliseg near Llangollen (early ninth century). On it he was listed, along with Vortigern, among the ancestors of the dynasty of Powys as 'Maximus rex qui occidit regem Romanorum', 'Maximus the king who killed the king of the Romans'. The tenth-century Harleian genealogies presented him, *Maxim guletic* – 'Maxen the ruler' – as the ancestor of the kingdoms of Dyfed (in this case incorporating him into the family of Constantine and his mother Helena, who will be discussed below) and the Isle of Man (as 'Maxim guletic qui occidit Gratianum regem Romanorum', 'Maxim the ruler who killed Gratian, king of the Romans'). Minor variants and late additions to the genealogical material connected him to the ancestors of the south-east kingdom of Gwynllwg and, evidently through error, one of the royal lineages of Dál Riata, the early west-Scottish kingdom, in whose genealogy he was described as *amherawdyr Ruuein*, 'Roman emperor'. Maxen also appeared in the genealogies of various saints. The title that he sometimes bore, *gwledic*, seemed to have some particular significance, being applied to characters whose stories were located in the Roman or immediate post-Roman period, including Emrys, Ceredig and Cunedda.

Under the name Macsen, Maximus also figured as an important founding ancestor in a self-contained tale, *Breudwyt Macsen Wledic* (another of the eleven tales making up the Mabinogion collection). The tale is as difficult to date as the other tales of the collection; the most recent suggestions would locate it in the mid-thirteenth century. Geoffrey of Monmouth's account of this character, whom he called Maximianus, was closely related to this tale. The relationship between the two has been heavily debated, with arguments giving anteriority if not outright influence to each in turn. It is probably fair to say that both Geoffrey and the author of *Breudwyt Macsen* probably drew on the same original. The fact that Geoffrey's version was the less embellished of the two could be taken as evidence that his was more faithful to a posited original. Equally, it could be attributed to Geoffrey's interest in events at the expense of description or other literary flourishes. Both versions, however, had as a central theme the close links between the rulers of Rome and Britain, these figures embodying continuity between Roman and post-Roman Britain and the close connection of the foundation of Brittany to this theme.

Geoffrey placed the story of Maximianus (as he called him) in a context close to that of the historical Magnus Maximus. In his version, the Roman senator Constantius seized the crown of Britain after the death of the usurping ruler of Britain, Coel, duke of Colchester, and married Coel's daughter Helena (Bk v.6). Constantius died in York and bequeathed his kingdom to his son, Constantinus, who marched on Rome and defeated the dictator Maxentius, becoming emperor. Apart from Helena's British roots and the name of her father Coel, this was unremarkable in historical terms. Then Geoffrey introduced Octavius, duke of the *Gewissei*, who seized the throne of Britain, keeping it despite several defeats at the hands of Helena's uncles. In old age Octavius could not decide how to dispose of his kingdom and his sole child, a daughter (unnamed), the choices being marrying her to a Roman or to Conanus Meriadocus, his nephew. Caradocus, the duke of Cornwall, advised that Octavius's daughter should be married to the Roman senator Maximianus, who was of British descent on his father's side and of Roman descent on his mother's side. Geoffrey made it clear that Maximianus 'was of royal blood on both sides [i.e. British and Roman]' (Bk v.9). This discomfited Conanus, who then tried to seize the kingship by force. Octavius sought the help of Maximianus, who was somewhat at leisure having been denied a third share of the Roman emperorship by the two emperors, Gratianus and Valentinianus. Maximianus was persuaded to help Octavius partly by being reminded that in the past Britain was often a place in which Romans could retrench in order to capture Rome, 'just as your kinsman Constantine did and many other kings of ours [i.e. British kings] who became emperors' (Bk v.9). Octavius, however, mistook Maximianus for an invading Roman, and sent Conanus to fight him, but then they made peace. Maximianus married Octavius's daughter and gained the crown. He later invaded Gaul, defeating the Armoricans and Franks, and promised Conanus the rule of Gaul in compensation for being deprived of the kingship of Britain. Maximianus's savagery resulted in the need for a repopulation of Armorica from Britain, over which Conanus was ruling. The episode is needlessly bloody with respect to several different characters and events: Geoffrey criticized the savagery of Maximianus and Conanus; moreover, shiploads of women from Britain, intended to help populate Brittany, were gratuitously killed by pirates (here Geoffrey was embellishing the legend of St Ursula and the 11,000 virgins, although apparently without mentioning Ursula's name, at least according to most manuscripts). Maximianus, having denuded Britain of troops, had left her open to invasion by the Picts and Huns who then committed mayhem until driven off by reinforcements from Maximianus. Maximianus was finally killed by friends of Gratianus. Britain descended into chaos, with invasions by the returning Picts and Huns, joined by Scots,

Norwegians and Danes (Bk vi.1). Rome sent more troops, but these were ultimately forced to depart, the Romans somewhat anticipating Napoleon when they noted that the Britons who were left in Britain were 'commoners ignorant of war and concerned with other matters, such as tilling the fields and various enterprises of trade' (Bk vi.2). Britain ultimately sought a new king among the descendants of Conanus in Brittany.

Again, Geoffrey's account was thus strikingly close to that of *Historia Brittonum*. Geoffrey's Maximianus had two main characteristics: he was the one who took Roman troops from Britain, with disastrous effect, and he presided over the founding of Brittany from Britain. *Breudwyt Macsen* was different in its additions and its omissions. *Breudwyt Macsen* set its events in a relatively timeless setting – albeit a notionally pre-Roman one with Roman emperors in Rome and British kings in Britain. It described how the Roman emperor Maxen had a vision of a maiden who was then found in Britain. She, rather dismissively, told Maxen's men that Maxen must seek her himself, a demand that brought Maxen to Britain. In coming to Britain, Maxen conquered the island by defeating Beli son of Manogan (i.e. Beli Mawr) and his sons, an act hurried over in one sentence. The maiden was identified as Elen Lluydauc, 'Elen of the Hosts', daughter of Eudaf Hen and sister of Cynan. Elen gained from Maxen as her maiden fee the Island of Britain for her father and built many roads. Maxen tarried so long in Britain that he had to re-conquer Rome. After a year of trying to conquer Rome, however, Maxen and his Roman troops were forced to wait outside while Cynan and his British troops fought inside the city, one part fighting with the Romans and another part barring the city from Maxen's troops. Only after three days and complete victory did Cynan hand the city over to Maxen once he asked for it: again the tale stressed that this was the men of the Island of Britain in whose power this gift lay. Cynan and the British were then set loose to gain what realm they might by conquest: they end up in what was later revealed to be Brittany. The story went on to give an account of the colonization of Brittany which was fuller (if also more contrived) than that in *Historia Brittonum*, including an onomastic legend. This purported to explain Llydaw, the Welsh name for Brittany as derived from the words *lled*, 'half' and *taw*, 'silent', because the British slew all the men of Brittany and cut out the tongues of the women lest the British speech be corrupted. The point of the tale, apart from its literary embellishments, was the continuity of British rulership of Roman Britain, augmented by British rule of Rome, accomplished through the relationship through marriage of these significant figures, Maxen and the family of Elen and Cynan. Along with this went the foundation of Brittany. In the tale, Maxen's position and actions vis-à-vis both Rome and Britain were entirely legitimate. His departure from Britain was accomplished without criticism and there was no sense that his rule of Britain was compromised. In particular, no one invaded Britain because of his absence. We seem to have references to a tale similar to *Breudwyt Maxen* in the triad 'Three Levies that departed from this Island, and not one of them came back' (no. 35, discussed above) in which one of the three is the one departing with Elen Lluydavc and her brother Cynan – it doesn't specify where they went. A later version added Maxen to Elen's host and added that they went to *Llychlyn*, which usually refers to Scandinavia but is probably here a corruption of *Llydaw*, Brittany.

There are significant differences between *Breudwyt Maxen* and Geoffrey's *Historia*. Geoffrey did not tell the story of the cutting out of the Bretons' tongues, although it could be argued that this tale may have lain behind Geoffrey's needlessly violent account of the attempt to send women to Brittany. More importantly, Geoffrey did not name Octavius's daughter. The tale's naming of Maxen's wife would seem to be its own innovation. Her name, Elen Lluydauc, which only appears part way through the tale in connection with road building, is extremely suggestive. The tenth-century genealogy of the rulers of Dyfed in Harleian 3859 that mentions Maxen also mentions, seven generations earlier, Helen, the mother of Constantine the Great, 'who went from Britain as far as Jerusalem in order to seek the cross of Christ and then took it to Constantinople, where it lies even today'. This is a reference to St Helena, mother of Constantine, who reputedly found the True Cross – a story circulating soon after her death. In this genealogy she was given the epithet *luitdauc* which she also bore in the translations of

Geoffrey's *Historia Regum Britanniae* into Welsh and which was that given to Elen in *Breudwyt Maxen*. This genealogy was the earliest evidence of the attribution of British origins to St Helena, origins that although unsupported by the historical record were reasonable enough in view of the associations of both Constantius, her husband, and Constantine the Great, her son, with Britain. She figured in several Welsh and Breton genealogies as an ancestress, although she was not usually said in these sources to have been British herself.

A genealogy in the Breizo-Latin *Life of St Gurthiern* (composed in its extant form in the 1120s but using earlier materials) described Helena, the finder of the True Cross, as the ancestress of *Outham Senis* (this is probably the form lying behind Geoffrey's Octavius, perhaps misread as Octham) and of Maximinanus, but did not explicitly associate her with Britain. In these Brythonic genealogies, she is always the mother of Constantine, and if her husband is named he is Constantius; she is never Maxen's British wife, although perhaps this idea is what lay behind an extremely confused genealogy of St Cadog found in Oxford, Jesus College MS 20. This genealogy pauses several times to relate stories concerning its items, a habit that significantly interrupts its ability to assemble a coherent list of generations. Its list contains, for example, at least two Maxens, the first of which was king of the British but then became emperor of Rome, with Cynan taking his place as British king – we will return to Cynan below. Elen 'Luedyawc' was in this genealogy mother of Constantine and bringer of part of the True Cross to Constantinople and another part to Britain. There is no direct connection with Maxen, except that Elen seems to have another son, Owain. The next item in the genealogy is the descent of an Owain (the same?), from (a different?) Maxen and Ceindrech, who herself is descended from Caswallon, whose story is told as well. This is a very distracted account, one whose genealogical rigour is a poor second to its storytelling. If we understand it to be making Elen and Maxen the parents of Owein (and this would contradict its statement that Ceindrech and Maxen were his parents), it would be only one of two places, outside *Breudwyt Maxen*, where Maxen's wife was named. The other, a genealogical text giving the descent of various saints and dating from the twelfth century or later, *Bonedd y Saint*, names St Peblic as the son of Maxen and Elen. A later version of this tract, *Achau'r Saint*, gives only Maxen as Peblic's father. In every other case, apart from *Breudwyt Maxen*, Maxen's wife is unnamed.

St Helena's British associations were unmentioned, apart from the tenth-century Harleian genealogy and the Jesus College genealogy discussed above, until the twelfth century, when the Anglo-Norman writer Henry of Huntingdon described her as the daughter of Coel, whom he described as the eponymous king of Colchester (*Historia Anglorum*, i.37). Henry was the first person to name Coel as Helena's father and thus grandfather of Constantine the Great; presumably, he was reporting an existing and entirely predictable (and, needless to say, false) etymology – if he were Geoffrey we might suspect that he invented Coel himself. Geoffrey adopted and embellished this story, derived either from Henry or from his source. The Welsh translators of Geoffrey transformed Coel into Iarll Caerloyw, 'earl of Gloucester', and in the fifteenth century he was conflated with a Coel who had a much older and more significant genealogical status, Coel Hen or Coel Godebog. This conflated Coel of Colchester/Gloucester was integrated into other genealogical texts. The Harleian genealogy aside, then, it would seem to be through Coel that Helena joined a series of Brythonized Roman characters, mostly historical in their origins although not in their subsequent guises. Neither Henry nor Geoffrey mentioned the True Cross.

This Helena, the mother of Constantine, seems to have been a separate character from the (mostly unnamed) wife of Maxen as far as medieval Welsh tradition was concerned. Nonetheless, both fulfilled a similar role in linking Roman figures to Britain by marriage. This is not a unique tendency: we have already noted the genealogy of St Cadog found in Jesus College MS 20, which piled up Roman and Christian associations by stating that Anna, the Virgin Mary's cousin, was not only Beli Mawr's mother – she was elsewhere described as his wife – but was also the daughter of a Roman emperor. In these schemes, St Helena was a significant ancestress; however, Maximianus and his (unnamed, but clearly not Coel's daughter nor Constantine's mother Helena) wife in Geoffrey's scheme did not have any issue. This was logical in view of Geoffrey's presentation of Maximianus as a usurper and contributor to Britain's weakness. Likewise, *Breudwyt Maxen* did not say whether Elen and Maxen had children.

Eudaf Hen, Elen's father according to *Breudwyt Maxen*, seems to have made his earliest Welsh appearance in *Breudwyt Maxen*, although he probably lay behind the Outham named in the *Life of Gurthiern*, an earlier source from Brittany – as we noted above, Geoffrey's own source probably also had the form Outham. The translators of Geoffrey's *Historia* into Welsh rendered his Octavius as Eudaf, making a straightforward equivalence. Cynan, Conan or Conanus (as Geoffrey has him), son of Eudaf, was not mentioned in *Historia Brittonum*, although the colonization of Brittany was. Cynan was assigned a more significant role by such Breton sources as we have. He appeared in the *Life of St Gurthiern* as a brother of Beli, both sons of Outham Senis; Cynan, the *Life* says, ruled Britain when the Britons went to Rome and took Brittany. This is a clear reference to the story of Maxen, which combined the idea that Britons left Britain for Rome and founded Brittany at the same time, but Maxen is not mentioned in the Breton text. Another medieval Latin text of Breton origin, the *Life of St Goueznou*, gave Conan the surname Meriadoc and told the story of the cutting out of tongues, again without mentioning Maxen. The nature of this episode's relationship to Geoffrey's *Historia* is debatable, although scholarly opinion has cautiously agreed that it probably pre-dated Geoffrey. If so, it was the earliest text to assign the surname 'Meriadoc' to Cynan/Conan, and to refer to the colonization of Brittany by the Britons with its mutilation of tongues. Later, Breton historians adopted Conan as the first king of Brittany. The extent to which we should see Geoffrey's influence here is debatable: the *Life of St Goueznou* and the *Life of Gurthiern* appear to show that such portrayal of Conan was a pre-Geoffrey tradition. The question of Geoffrey's use, or creation, of 'traditional' material is as difficult to establish with respect to the Breton material as it is to establish with respect to the Welsh material.

The figure of Cynan or Conan brings up one final, very important question as regards Geoffrey's relationship to 'traditional' Welsh historical writing: that of Cynan's role as a saviour who was expected to return to preside over the righting of wrongs. The poem *Armes Prydein Fawr*, 'The Great Prophecy of Britain', probably dating from the tenth century, cited Cynan and Cadwaladr several times as those who would return to lead an unrealistically large pan-Celtic and Viking army against the Saxons on behalf of the British. The poem is difficult to date in part because it obscures its specific political context with a mix of speculation and wishful thinking. Neither Cynan nor Cadwaladr had any identifying features in the poem, although as the Bretons are included it is entirely reasonable to expect that Cynan might equate to Conan Meriadoc. If we keep in mind that allusion was the main literary technique used by medieval Welsh poetry to provide points of reference, the fact that *Armes Prydein* refers to Cynan and Cadwaladr in the briefest terms could be taken as a sign that their stories (whether individual or joint) were already well known. Certainly, at least one other poem from the Book of Taliesin, *Glaswawt Taliesin*, cited them jointly in a similar role to that of *Armes Prydein*. Material from the Black Book of Carmarthen, to be discussed below with respect to Myrddin, also cited them in this fashion.

In our earliest sources originating from Wales (*Historia Brittonum*, early ninth century) and Brittany (the *Life of St Gurthiern*, which may considerably pre-date its writing down in the 1120s), we find the view that colonization of Brittany from Britain left Britain vulnerable. Even more, then, would it make sense to have one of her saviours, Cynan or Conan, come from there. Certainly this was Geoffrey's view: the prophecies in *Historia Regum Britanniae* (Bk vii.3) implied that the prophesied Conanus (with no surname) would come from Brittany, and *Vita Merlini* (discussed below) said so explicitly (ll. 964–8). Geoffrey very probably knew *Armes Prydein* and incorporated its statements that Cynan and Cadwaladr would come to save Britain. This is not to say that Geoffrey did adapt his material, however: his emphasis on the importance of the Bretons to British history goes well beyond his Welsh source material.

We know even less about the Cadwaladr of this prophetic tradition than we do about Cynan, despite his important role. The Welsh genealogical material provides several Cadwaladrs to choose from. The best known, and the one probably in question in the prophecies, was Cadwaladr son of Cadwallon, relatively well attested in historical terms as ruler of Gwynedd in the seventh century. It has been argued that Cadwaladr was perceived as the last 'king' of Wales, with his successors merely 'princes'; this claim is not supported by the texts themselves, which do not differentiate in such terms between those who ruled before and after Cadwaladr. These include the poem of dialogue between Myrddin and his sister Gwenddydd (*Cyfoesi Myrddin a Gwenddydd ei Chwaer*), which includes a list of such rulers but does not distinguish between those ruling up to Cadwaladr and those ruling after. Certainly Geoffrey didn't make such a claim: while he ended *Historia Regum Britanniae* with the statement that the Welsh 'never afterwards recovered the overlordship (*monarchia*) of the island', he left 'the task of describing their [subsequent] kings (*reges*)' to a contemporary historian, Caradoc of Llancarfan, and those kings (*reges*) of the Saxons to William of Malmesbury and Henry of Huntingdon (Bk xii.20). He ended by referring to those about whom he was writing as both kings (*reges*) and princes (*principes*). Thus, there is no clear sign that Cadwaladr was particularly significant in medieval Welsh tradition, apart from his putative mention in company with Cynan as a returning leader. Still less clear is whether the existence of a team of two saviours, Cynan and Cadwaladr, was intended to represent the British in Brittany (Cynan) and the British at home (Cadwaladr). It may be coincidence that these two figures could be taken as such representatives of a dual Brythonic past: elsewhere in medieval Welsh tradition the foundation of Brittany was a tale with no particular sequel – it was a part of a larger, British picture; nothing more. Geoffrey, however, notably augmented the implicit significance of this – Brittany was founded just as British sovereignty was beginning to come under attack. This culminated, for Geoffrey, in the last British king, Cadualadrus, in exile in Brittany, being warned by the angelic voice not to return to Britain from Brittany, as God did not wish the Britons to rule Britain 'until the time came which Merlin had foretold to Arthur' (Bk xii.17). Although the angelic voice promised that the British would rule the island again in future, this was not specifically connected to the return of a named leader.

Cynan's and Cadwaladr's roles as prophesied saviours of Britain dominated the large body of medieval Welsh material concerned with prophecy. The figure so familiar to later medieval and modern English audiences, Arthur the redeemer, is not found in medieval Welsh texts of this sort, despite the fact that outside observers in the twelfth century said that the medieval Cornish, Bretons and Welsh believed that he would return. Yet, in other roles, Arthur clearly was increasingly popular in medieval Welsh literary circles, as much so as in other Latin and vernacular literary traditions – this was due, to a large part, to Geoffrey.

7

The Arthurian Section of
Historia Regum Britanniae

We have, so far, observed the complexity of Geoffrey's relations with the Welsh tradition. It is with the figures of Arthur and Merlin, however, that we see him working most actively in the formation of a new tradition. The Arthurian sections are the most read of Geoffrey's *Historia*. One segment, the *Prophetiae Merlini*, 'The Prophecies of Merlin', had an earlier circulation independent of the *Historia*, while Merlin was the subject of Geoffrey's final work, the *Vita Merlini*, 'Life of Merlin'.

According to *Historia Regum Britanniae*, after the great disaster that was Maximianus's reign and with the final departure of the Roman troops and invaders descending upon Britain, Geoffrey's Britons looked to Brittany to supply a king, Constantinus. At Constantinus's death, Vortigern, a cunning usurper of uncertain origin – like Octavius, he belonged to the obscure *Gewissei* – persuaded Constantine's youngest son, Constans, to become king. Vortigern then insinuated his way into the affections of the Picts and persuaded them to kill Constans. Under threat from the Picts and the British, Vortigern welcomed the pagan Horsus and Hengest. Leaving aside King Constans, this is more or less the story briefly related in *Historia Brittonum*, which had its climax in the disclosure of the red and white dragons. As noted above, Geoffrey made a crucial substitution in this episode: he turned the boy seer of *Historia Brittonum* from Ambrosius or Emrys into Merlin, although Geoffrey noted that Merlin 'was also called Ambrosius' (Bk vi.19) and used the form 'Ambrosius Merlin' twice (Bks vi.19 and vii.3). Geoffrey greatly diminished the role of St Germanus as critic of Vortigern as it was in *Historia Brittonum* – in which text Germanus criticized Vortigern for personal sin rather than political wrongdoing. In *Historia Regum Britanniae*, Germanus appeared during Vortigern's reign, but only to preach against Pelagianism. Thus, Merlin's explanation that the story of the dragons represented Vortigern's grave error in inviting the Saxons to Britain – the only public criticism of Vortigern in Geoffrey's *Historia* – focused on his political wrongdoing rather than on his personal wickedness, as in *Historia Brittonum* (Bk viii.1).

The discovery of the dragons led to a prophetic interlude, which incorporated the *Prophetiae Merlini*, an earlier work of Geoffrey's that occurred within the *Historia* but with its own preface and dedication, and which was quoted extensively by Orderic Vitalis's *Ecclesiastical History* in 1135, at least a year, if not several, before *Historia Regum Britanniae* was finished. In his preface to the *Prophetiae*, Geoffrey claimed (as he did in the preface to the *Historia*) to be translating 'from British into Latin' (Bk vii.2). This claim has been greeted with the same scepticism as that in the preface of the *Historia*: the prophecies are now regarded as Geoffrey's own invention, although probably drawing to some extent on an existing prophetic tradition in Welsh. We will consider the figure of Merlin further below.

After the prophetic interlude, Vortigern fled and the brothers of the rightful ruler, Constans, returned from Brittany (Bk viii.1): these were Aurelius Ambrosius and Uther Pendragon. Geoffrey derived Aurelius from both Gildas and *Historia Brittonum*: in the former he was a successful leader against the Saxons before the period marked by the battle of Badon Hill, and in the latter he was directly, if somewhat obscurely, connected with Vortigern's fall. Geoffrey devoted some time to Aurelius. Aurelius presided over a period of victory, peace and rebuilding. In pursuit of an appropriate monument to British princes treacherously massacred by Hengest and buried at a monastery near Salisbury founded by Ambrius (Bk vi.15, embellishing ch. 46 of *Historia Brittonum*), Ambrosius was directed to Merlin, who had expertise in both prophecy and engineering (Bk viii.10). Merlin refused to provide more prophecies, but he did suggest a fitting monument: the 'Giants' Ring' of Ireland, the stones of which had magical and medicinal properties (Bk viii.11). Merlin was instrumental in helping to move these stones, which could not be shifted by ordinary means, although the extent to which supernatural powers rather than sophisticated knowledge were involved is unclear. The resulting monument was near Ambrius's monastery, presumably standing for Amesbury. Ambrius himself is almost certainly Geoffrey's invention, a back-formation from Ambresburia – we might note that Geoffrey thus gave this Anglo-Saxon monastery a British founder. The monument itself was almost certainly meant to be Stonehenge, although Geoffrey did not name it. He located it at Amesbury itself rather than several miles away as would be appropriate for Stonehenge, and was somewhat unclear as to its exact form apart from its being circular (was he thinking of Avebury?). At the death of Aurelius, a portent was seen and Merlin was summoned to interpret it. He explained that Aurelius had died, Uther was to become king and Uther's son Arthur (who was not, however, named) was to rule Britain and beyond (Bk viii.15). Uther developed a passion for Igerna, the wife of Gorlois, duke of Cornwall (and Uther's advisor). He enlisted Merlin's help to disguise himself as Gorlois and visited Igerna at Tintagel, at which point Arthur was conceived (Bk viii.19). This was Merlin's last appearance in the *Historia*: he never met Arthur himself. The earliest account of such a meeting was in Robert de Boron's metrical romance *Merlin*, generally dated to the late twelfth century.

Arthur's career clearly was the high point of the *Historia Regum Britanniae* and certainly is its best-known section. The account of his reign occupied about one-fifth of the *Historia*, far more than Geoffrey devoted to any other character. This was partly due to the fact that Arthur had many adventures so that the enumeration of his deeds took up a lot of space. His career began with three of the twelve battles attributed to him in *Historia Brittonum*, which Geoffrey embellished and located near York, Lincoln and Bath (Bk ix.1–5). The last of these battles, which clearly was intended as Badon Hill, mentioned by Gildas, had the effect of entirely conquering the Saxons: a reflection, if embellished, of Gildas's view of the decisiveness of this battle. Arthur quickly routed the Scots and the Picts, after which there followed a golden age of rebuilding similar to that undertaken by Ambrosius, although it was not marked by the erection of a monument as significant as Stonehenge. Arthur married Guinevere (whose name is spelled in different ways depending on the manuscript), who was said to be descended from a Roman family, and set off to conquer the islands closest to Britain: Ireland, Iceland, Gotland and Orkney. After a brief digression on the nobility and fame of Arthur's court (a topic to which Geoffrey later returned), Arthur set off on another series of foreign conquests, these ones further from Britain. In this he was inspired by a somewhat self-fulfilling logic: other nations heard of Arthur's fame and prepared themselves for his invasion; these preparations spurred him to attempt their conquest, of which Gaul was the most notable (Bk ix.11). The implication of Arthur's position is that his need for further conquest derived from his need to maintain his generosity to his followers, but this does put him in an awkward position when it came time to defend Britain against unjust exactions of tribute, gained by conquest, demanded by Rome. Before this happened, however, Geoffrey paused, somewhat uncharacteristically, to describe Arthur's plenary court at Caerleon, a city founded, appropriately, by Belinus, a Briton who conquered Rome.

It seems probable that Geoffrey chose to locate Arthur's court, which in Welsh tradition was located at 'Celli Wic in Cornwall', at Caerleon partly because of his origins in the region and partly because of Caerleon's impressive Roman remains, which could serve as an important reminder of Britain's Roman links. Geoffrey described the city at length, noting its history, including the martyrdom of Julius and Aaron mentioned by Gildas (*De Excidio Britanniae*, ch. x.2). He included long lists of those invited to the court, who assembled for love of Arthur (Bk ix.12). Ceremonies, masses and feasts were referred to, with Geoffrey breaking off to note that,

> If I were to describe it all in detail, my history would become too wordy. So noble was Britain then that it surpassed other kingdoms in its stores of wealth, the ostentation of its dress and the sophistication of its inhabitants.

Tournaments ensued, at which point Geoffrey indulged again uncharacteristically in a description of the women's courtly behaviour. The distribution of ecclesiastical benefices in Britain and Brittany ensued, and finally a contingent of envoys arrived from Rome with a letter from Lucius Hiberius, procurator of the Roman Republic. Lucius brusquely demanded that Arthur come to Rome to answer for his behaviour: his withholding of Britain's tribute and his conquest of Roman possessions. As Arthur and the assembled rulers withdrew to consider this, Cador, duke of Cornwall, rejoiced that they could now abandon their games and dalliances with women and return to their proper pursuit, which was battle. Arthur then gave what must be, in the light of his own activities, an unconvincing account of how tyranny and conquest could not be justified, purporting to be relying on legal principles in asserting that the Roman demand for tribute could only be answered with a British demand for Roman tribute (Bk ix.16). If conquest justified tribute, Arthur continued, he could cite numerous examples of British conquerors of Rome, including Belinus and Brennius, Constantinus and Maximianus ('close relations of mine'). Hoel, king of Brittany, echoed Arthur's arguments, citing a Sibylline prophecy that three Britons should rule Rome, the first two being Belinus and Constantinus. Everyone agreeing, Arthur prepared to depart, leaving his nephew Modred and his queen Guinevere to maintain Britain in his absence.

Geoffrey injected a note of foreboding as Arthur had a dream involving a bear and a dragon which was clearly prophetic, but the import of which was unclear (Bk x.2). Another episode digressed somewhat from the march to Rome, as Arthur and his companions slew a giant at Mont-Saint-Michel. This episode, which served as a reminder of the Cornishmen's Trojan ancestor Corineus (a giant-killer), contained a story within a story, concerning another giant, Retho, also slain by Arthur. These episodes slow Geoffrey's otherwise brisk advance of events, and while Arthur moved then to battle with the Romans in Gaul, the battle itself bogged down somewhat, occupying several days and nine chapters (Bk x.4–12). Nevertheless, the Britons were victorious, and Lucius himself was killed, his body being sent to the Roman senate as a reply to the request for tribute. Arthur tarried in Gaul, preparing to march to Rome, but then heard of Modred's usurpation of his rule and his wife. At this point, Geoffrey cited Walter, archdeacon of Oxford, as his authority and addressed himself to his *consul augustus*, that is, his patron, declaring his intention not to relate what happened next, apparently because of its unhappy nature. There is considerable manuscript variation here, and some readings suggest the opposite, that Geoffrey did promise to press on, presumably to relate Arthur's unhappy end. The former reading seems preferable.

At any rate, Geoffrey's narrative makes little of Guinevere's adultery and much of Modred's usurpation of the crown: Geoffrey was interested in the political significance of the event (one whose contemporary relevance, however, remains unclear) and had little time for the personal dimension that would come to mean so much to romance writers in the French tradition. Arthur and Modred met at the River Camblan in Cornwall where Modred was killed and Arthur fatally wounded, but Arthur was taken to the Isle of Avalon to have his wounds seen to. Geoffrey would have found references to the battle of Camlan in the Welsh annals, which stated under the year 537 that Arthur and Medraut fell in battle there. The location, like that of all Arthur's purported battles, is obscure: Geoffrey's location of it in Cornwall may have relied on local Cornish tradition or, more probably, may have stemmed from a desire to bring Arthur, the 'Boar of Cornwall', full circle to where he was conceived, the River Camel being only four miles from Tintagel. Geoffrey seems to have been the first to associate Arthur with both sites, although Arthur's associations with Cornwall in general are certainly older than Geoffrey.

It is perhaps worth pausing to consider, briefly, these Cornish connections. The medieval Welsh tale *Culhwch ac Olwen*, as well as several of the Welsh triads, gave the location of Arthur's court as 'Celli Wic in Cornwall'. Geoffrey changed this to Caerleon but gave prominence to Cornwall in other ways: at the settlement of Britain, Brutus and his sons were eponyms of the island and its constituent regions: Loegria, Kambria, Albania. Cornwall apparently did not form part of any of these, being the region of its eponymous founder Corineus, a companion rather than a son of Brutus. In administrative terms, Geoffrey often showed Cornwall as standing apart from Britain's component kingdoms. The dukes of Cornwall were advisors to British rulers, as well as being a source of brides and rulers when an existing ruling line failed. Arthur himself was son of Igerna, duchess of Cornwall, and was husband of Guinevere, daughter of his close advisor Cador, duke of Cornwall; he was clearly intended to be the Boar of Cornwall in Merlin's prophecies. Geoffrey seems to have been relatively well acquainted with places and local events in Cornwall, Tintagel being the most notable but certainly not the only example. Geoffrey gave Arthur's nephew, Modredus, a name in a Cornish (or Breton) form rather than in the Welsh form Medraut, which is found in *Annales Cambriae*, presumably Geoffrey's main source for this episode. Moreover, the name itself was known in several examples from medieval Cornish and Breton sources; the name is unknown in the Welsh material apart from our Arthurian Medraut, who was also mentioned several times by medieval poets and seems to appear in several genealogies. This raises the possibility that Medraut might have been of Cornish (or Breton) origin, a possibility strengthened by Geoffrey's use of the Cornish form of the name, almost certainly from a source supplementing *Annales Cambriae*.

While Geoffrey's interest in Arthur was unmistakable, it is striking that Arthur in the *Historia Regum Britanniae* was for the most part presented as one element in the large-scale picture of British history rather than as an individual character with over-riding importance. For Geoffrey, arguably, the whole picture was more important than any one particular element. Like other characters in the *Historia*, Arthur had no individual personality as such – as illustrated, for example, in his lack of reaction to the revelation of his wife's adultery. This is in keeping with Geoffrey's lack of interest in personalities. No one person really bears the weight of the whole of British history; no one character achieves individual significance even as a driver of events. Arthur, however, did provide a useful link between the two main phases of the *Historia Regum Britanniae*, between the Roman/British period and the Saxon/ Welsh period. It is important, however, not to allow what later writers made of Geoffrey and the enthusiasm with which they took up Arthur in particular to lead us to forget the relative austerity of Geoffrey's account of Arthur. Although he was given a full biography by Geoffrey, including a magical conception and elements that appeared in later romance portraits, such as friends, a court, etc., he had not yet been embellished to the extent that he would be by later medieval writers. Nor did Geoffrey's Arthur have many of our modern Arthur's characteristic possessions, companions and attributes, such as the round table.

As far as *Historia Regum Britanniae* was concerned, whatever Arthur's merits, the inexorable slide downhill for the Britons began with the settlement of Brittany, a fact highlighted by the increasing recourse of British leaders, including Arthur, to help from Brittany. These appeals were frequently accompanied by musings on Britain's plight now that she was devoid of her strongest men. This aspect of *Historia Regum Britanniae* has, not surprisingly, fed arguments as to Geoffrey's own identity. While it is clear that in chronological terms the settlement of Brittany marked the beginning of the end for the British, if we look at it from an author's point of view, it is clear that if Geoffrey was to present the loss of British sovereignty as an ambivalent and open-ended process, as he clearly wished to do, the notion of British heroism being diverted elsewhere was a useful one. Moreover, it was, arguably, inherent in the medieval Welsh historiographical tradition which, while it concentrated on the fall of Roman Britain and the ensuing, catastrophic Anglo-Saxon settlement, also linked the foundation of Brittany to these events.

Arthur did not merely (or even?) die: he was defeated by internal rather than external foes (no doubt Gildas would nod knowingly here) before he was able to accomplish his goal, a goal that had already been achieved by his predecessors. Even the question of Arthur's return to redeem the British was rendered obscure: mortally wounded (*letaliter uulneratus*), he was carried off to the Isle of Avalon so that his wounds might be healed (*ad sananda uulnera sua*). Later, at the end of the story, the Angelic Voice stopped Cadualadrus from returning from his Breton exile to come to the aid of the Welsh by saying that the British would not be sovereign in Britain until the moment should come that Merlin prophesied to, or perhaps for, Arthur (Bk xii.17). The question as to what that moment might consist of was also deliberately left obscure. Arthur never met Merlin – therefore, Merlin could not, strictly speaking, have prophesied anything *to* him – thus, we might imagine that the voice might have been referring to a prophecy *about* him, which Merlin had indeed produced, if we see Arthur as the Boar of Cornwall of the prophecies. Subsequently, in his *Vita Merlini*, Geoffrey made the matter clearer: here, we have the earliest direct reference to Arthur's return. In a conversation between Telgesinus (that is, Geoffrey's version of Taliesin) and Merlin, the former described how he bore Arthur to the Island of Apples where Morgen promised to heal him, noting that this would, however, take a long time. Telgesinus suggested that Arthur be brought back in order to lead the Britons to victory, but Merlin stated that this would be premature: victory would be achieved later, through an alliance of Scots, Welsh, Cornish and Bretons led by Conanus and Cadualadrus (*Vita Merlini*, ll. 930–75). This of course is almost exactly the scenario offered by *Armes Prydein*.

Probably the most obscure aspect of the question of how much of Geoffrey's account of Arthur was taken from his sources and how much he invented is this matter of Arthur's return. In this context, we should consider the account of canons from Laon on a fund-raising tour through Britain in 1113 as narrated by one Hermann (of Tournai, probably). Hermann's account describes a near-riot on the visit of the canons to Bodmin in Cornwall, as one of them expressed disbelief when a Cornishman insisted ('as the Bretons are wont to do', commented Hermann) that Arthur was not dead. This is one of the few indications that we have that Arthur's return may have been prophesied before Geoffrey's narrative became the normative expression of this idea. Another, whose import is however almost entirely obscure, is a statement in the Middle Welsh poem, *Englynion y Beddau*, that Arthur's grave is 'the world's wonder (*anoeth*)', the 'wonder' of it being, perhaps, that it was difficult to find. Other hints come not from Celtic but from Norman sources: William of Malmesbury commented (mid-1120s) that Arthur's grave could not be found and stated that 'fables' say that Arthur would return (*De Gestis Regum Anglorum*, i.1). This latter sentiment, attributed to the Welsh, is echoed in the Anglo-Norman poem, *Lestorie des Engles*, of *c*.1140.

The question clearly was a pressing one for the Angevins and their successors: in 1191, Arthur's body (and, according to some accounts, those of Guinevere and Modred as well) was 'discovered' at Glastonbury Abbey. Historians have long agreed that the purpose of this – almost certainly concocted – event was to illustrate the strength and legitimacy of Angevin rule over Wales, both by establishing that Arthur was indeed dead, and by associating his remains with the current kings of England, in this case Henry II (who, according to Gerald of Wales, suggested the excavation) and Richard I (the reigning monarch at the time of the discovery). Glastonbury had an active and imaginative antiquarian tradition, and the site was one of the candidates for the location of Avalon even before 1191. Angevin politics dictated the nature and characterization of the descriptions of the discoveries, including perhaps the presence or absence of Guinevere and Modred in various accounts. Various revisitations were carried out when the Welsh or the Scots were particularly restive. Edward I, in 1278, had presided over a second exhumation of Arthur's and Guinevere's remains at Glastonbury. In 1301, Edward wrote a letter to Boniface VII defending his claim to Scotland, citing in support of it Arthur's conquest of Scotland and the ensuing subjection of Scottish kings to British ones; the Scots were, not surprisingly, unconvinced. The famous round table at Winchester would seem to date from Edward I's reign as well, although its paintings date from considerably later.

Arthur was increasingly 'anglicized' and historicized; the two processes were closely related. Welsh rulers seemed not to have made such appeals to Arthurian tradition: our only example of an appeal to the past invoked not Arthur but Brutus. In 1282, one month before his death, Llywelyn ap Gruffudd cited the descent of the Britons from Brutus the Trojan in a letter to Archbishop Pecham rejecting proposals of surrender from Edward I. Surely, this referred to Geoffrey's *Historia*: we may note that it occurred several years before Edward's famous invocation of Brutus and his sons to Pope Boniface in defence of his actions in Scotland in 1301, which is often held to be a landmark in the use of legendary history in political debate. The Scots were able to counter Edward's Brutus with their own legendary ancestor, Scota, well known in medieval Irish origin-legends. This alternative to Galfredian history, a specific retort to Geoffrey's British history, dominated subsequent accounts of Scotland's origins.

In Wales, Geoffrey's vision of British history prevailed. However, this did not necessarily include Arthur. The Welsh writer Elis Gruffydd, in the mid-sixteenth century, commented with wounded patriotism that while the English criticized the Welsh for presumption about Arthur, 'they talk much more about him than we do', and attributed to the English the belief that Arthur will return again from the cave near Glastonbury where he was sleeping. Perhaps this is one more explanation for Arthur's absence from medieval Welsh prophetic poetry – having been turned into Arthur of the English, he would not do as a candidate for the redeemer of the Welsh from their oppressors. Although Henry VII (Henry Tudor) appointed a commission to examine the descent of his Welsh ancestor Owen from the ancient British kings, the resulting report was not said to mention Arthur (although surely he was implied) but did highlight Brutus. We should, however, note the fact that Henry named his first-born son Arthur, which perhaps signifies Henry's covering of all possible ground. This Arthur shared with other royal Arthurs (most notably Henry II's grandson, Arthur of Brittany) a life ending with shattering inconclusiveness.

8

Merlin, *Prophetiae Merlini* and *Vita Merlini*

Of all the figures dealt with by Geoffrey in his writings, Merlin is most visibly Geoffrey's creation. Clearly, he was based in part on traditional materials, but these materials are so fragmentary and so ambiguous that Geoffrey's own interpretation may have had a more far-reaching influence on our own understanding than has generally been recognized. We cannot be certain of the extent to which our present view of a Merlin figure was due to Geoffrey. Some of Geoffrey's innovations are obvious: the substitution of Merlin for Ambrosius in the dragon episode is one such case. However, our ability to separate Geoffrey's Merlin from a puta- tively earlier Welsh persona, 'Myrddin', has recently been called into question, for very good reasons. We are left facing the possi- bility that almost everything we think we know about Myrddin was a reflection of Geoffrey's inventive habit and its legacy in Welsh literature. The precise balance of the 'traditional' and 'adapted' aspects of Geoffrey's material has not been, and probably cannot be, established; we can only be sure of the fact that Geoffrey worked with some older sources, not of their nature or extent. Central to this question is the vast difference between the first and the second of Geoffrey's Merlins: the first the Merlin of *Historia Regum Britanniae* of the 1130s, and the second the Merlin of Geoffrey's *Vita Merlini*, a considerably later work, dated to 1148–51.

As noted above, the prophecies of Merlin, published separately as *Prophetiae Merlini*, also formed part of the *Historia Regum Britanniae*. Even within the *Historia* they had their own introduc- tion and dedication, and were arguably an interruption of the event-driven narrative of the *Historia*. *Prophetiae Merlini* must have been composed and circulating by 1135 – as previously noted, in this year Orderic Vitalis quoted them at length, apparently as a separate text, in his *Historia Ecclesiastica* (Bk xii.47). They were very popular: there are eighty-five surviving manuscripts of the prophecies themselves in addition to the 200-odd manuscripts of *Historia Regum Britanniae*. In the *Historia*, Geoffrey led up to the prophecies by relating the story of the discovery of the red and white dragons. At that point, he substituted the name Merlin for the Ambrosius (Emrys) of the *Historia Brittonum*. He also located Merlin in Carmarthen, making his mother the daughter of the king of Demetia, Dyfed, in which region Carmarthen is located; *Historia Brittonum* concerned only Gwynedd.

The prophecies began with the identification of the red and white dragons, who were continually fighting as Merlin prophesied; the second prophecy foretold the ruin of religion and churches; the third prophecy stated in extremely general terms that the race oppressed 'will rise up and resist the foreigners' fury', with no mention of dragons. After that, we are told that the Boar of Cornwall (clearly Arthur) would bring relief. It is not made clear whether this is the final victory foretold in the preceding prophecy or merely a respite. If we were to read the prophecies as sequential, the respite would seem to have been brief as the next three prophecies seemed to tell the story of Arthur's life, and the fourth spoke of his successors. Various catastrophes were then prophesied. In a further prophecy, the 'Red One' would regain its strength, only, in yet a further prophecy, to 'return to its old ways and strive to tear at itself.'

A further prophecy seemed to begin where *Historia Regum Britanniae* left off. It stated that the white dragon would invite foreigners from Germany (presumably Vikings) and that the red dragon would 'languish at the pool's edge'. More conquerors (Normans?) were mentioned in a further prophecy, with one saying that they would enslave the people of the white dragon but treat the original inhabitants better – this would seem to be a rare nod on Geoffrey's part to a possible common cause between Britons and Normans, as enemies of the Saxons. Various symbolic birds, reptiles and animals were mentioned, including a 'dragon of Worcester' as well as a 'horned dragon' but the red and white dragons did not again appear. As Orderic Vitalis commented (*Historia Ecclesiastica*, Bk xii.4), the prophecies could more or less be followed up to the events of the present day, including some trenchant criticisms of Henry I. One prophecy mentioned events in Wales and Cornwall of the 1120s and 1130s ('Venedotia will run red with a mother's blood and the house of Corineus will kill six brothers'). The rest of the prophecies, being concerned with future events, were, not surprisingly, far more obscure. They included the statement that Cadualadrus and Conanus should ally with Scotland in order to slaughter the foreigners. After this Armorica would be 'crowned with Brutus's diadem. Kambria will be filled with rejoicing and the Cornish oaks will flourish. The island will be called by Brutus's name and the foreign term will disappear.' This is surely the fulfilment of the prophecy mentioned by the Angelic Voice at the end of the *Historia*, and it is notable that Cynan and Cadwaladr, not Arthur, presided over it, under circumstances similar to those described in *Armes Prydein*. In this, Geoffrey adhered quite strictly to Welsh tradition. However, his account was significantly different from that of *Historia Brittonum* in that the fulfilment of the main prophecy, the regaining of Britain by the British, was described in connection with Cynan, Cadwaladr and Brutus (and perhaps Arthur), and not in connection with the red dragon. The spirit was the same, but the details were significantly different. Moreover, Geoffrey's prophecies did not end with the British rightfully ruling Britain: they continued with a good deal of vague animal struggles and ended with the destruction of the world, whose description owed a great debt to the Book of Revelation.

The contemporary political content of these prophecies suggests that they are fully the work of Geoffrey. Those that followed the narrative trajectory of *Historia Regum Britanniae* were simply a continuation of its narrative into the future. As always with Geoffrey, the immense popularity of his own work and the production of further texts that it inspired serve to obscure the origins of any earlier material. Commenting on Geoffrey's prophetic material and supplementing it with reference to current political events were popular pastimes in the twelfth century. We find annotations in some of the manuscripts of the *Prophetiae*: these identify both well-attested historical events and those found only in Geoffrey's *Historia*. Prophecies held to be referring to events after Geoffrey's time were identified, such as Henry II's activities in Ireland from 1171 onwards, the settlement between John and Pope Innocent III of 1208–12 and the fall of William de Braose after 1208. The *Prophetiae* also provoked a hostile reaction by allies of Thomas Becket: in 1166, Herbert of Bosham cited one in a letter to Pope Alexander III, arguing that Henry II was using it to threaten Thomas Becket (Gerald of Wales revisited the prophecy after Becket's death in his *Expugnatio Hibernica*, 2.31.35). In a slightly different context, in a letter of 1169, John of Salisbury criticized Gilbert Foliot's claim that one of the prophecies supported London over Canterbury in terms of metropolitan status. We might note, however, that John had quoted with approval a different prophecy (to do with a tusked boar) in a letter to Thomas Becket in 1166. John concluded by deprecating his own interpretation of the prophecy, affecting to defer to Becket's Welsh clerk 'Alexander', whom he described as 'kin to Merlin and a more skilled interpreter of his prophecies'. Peter of Blois mentioned Merlin's prophecies in a commentary on Job of *c*.1173, but later claimed to have been making an ironic comment rather than endorsing the disreputable prophetic material. Various Norman and Anglo-Norman historians drew or commented on the prophecies, including Suger of Saint-Denis, Ralph de Diceto, Richard de Poitou and Étienne de Rouen. Interest in Merlin's prophecies extended well beyond the Norman world. In the thirteenth century, they were held to foretell the Holy Roman Emperor Frederick II (d.1250). The prophecies were translated into Icelandic in the early thirteenth century. A wave of interest in prophetic material in France in the fourteenth and fifteenth centuries attached itself in particular to Joan of Arc, with two of Geoffrey's prophecies being interpreted and revised as appropriate – at her trial Joan herself claimed that other people saw her as fulfilling one of these two prophecies, but that she herself did not credit it. Robert Ferrar, the often controversial Bishop of St Davids burned at the stake in Carmarthen in 1555, was said to have had such respect for his Welsh congregation that he cited

Merlin's prophecy that the Welsh would one day rule Britain once more, or so his enemies claimed (we should note that Arthur was not mentioned). In addition to such passing references there were also full-length commentaries.

That such writers were concerned with the contemporary relevance of the prophecies should not blind us to the fact that they did not respond only to Geoffrey's text but incorporated in their responses references to a wider genre of Welsh or British prophecy. Some of the commentaries, especially those emanating from 'Celtic' sources, were clearly drawing not only on Geoffrey's material, but also on material independent of Geoffrey. One suggestive text is a Latin poem on the prophecies of Merlin, composed in the mid-twelfth century (some time between 1141 and 1155) by John of Cornwall – a writer whose Cornish connections, despite his epithet, are obscure. One third of John's prophecies are taken from Geoffrey's, but some of the remaining material would seem to derive from Welsh prophetic poetry. John also added a prose commentary, containing Cornish place-names and words, as well as allusions to events in Cornwall. This does not necessarily point to a Cornish prophetic tradition, although it does show that the Welsh material could be accessed by a Latin writer, in addition to Geoffrey, in this case one who clearly had a good knowledge of Cornish. Indeed, John was recommended for the position of bishop of St Davids because of his knowledge of Welsh, a fact that counted against him in the final appointment.

Another, even more suggestive, collection of prophecies is that partially provided, and partially alluded to, by Gerald of Wales. In the first two books of his *Expugnatio Hibernica*, 'The Conquest of Ireland', completed about 1188, Gerald of Wales showed a significant interest in prophecy, referring to his history as a *vaticinalis historia*, 'prophetic history'. In the first two books of this work, Gerald quoted from two separate Merlins: one, 'Merlin Ambrosius', quoted on four occasions, was the Merlin of Geoffrey's *Prophetiae Merlini*; the second, 'Merlin Celidonius' or 'Merlin Silvester' (or even 'Merlin Silvester of Celidon'), quoted on ten occasions, provided material not found in Geoffrey's writings. Gerald repeatedly referred to a *Liber Vaticinorum*, 'Book of Prophecies', for additional information on these latter prophecies. This *Liber Vaticinorum* seemed to have been planned as a third volume which was to explain the prophecies of the Merlin Celidonius more fully. It was never completed or published – all we have is its preface. In it, Gerald described his project to publish the prophecies of Merlin Silvester of Celidon, preserved orally by British bards, which he says he translated (with help) from the British tongue, having found them in a book on the Llŷn Peninsula (in his *Itinerarium Kambriae*, Bk ii.6, he specified that he found them at Nefyn). In the preface, Gerald initially said that he was translating these prophecies at the request of Henry II, but then he abruptly announced that 'wise counsel' had decreed that the prophecies must not be published, lest they offend those in power. Gerald also seems to have expunged or edited the Merlin Silvester material in later versions of the *Expugnatio*, for reasons that are not clear. Gerald also included prophecies from 'Merlin Silvester' in his *Itinerarium Kambriae*, one of which, in Book i.6, echoes material from a Welsh prophetic poem, *Gwasgargerdd Fyrddin yn y Bedd*, found in the Red Book of Hergest as well as in the White Book of Rhydderch. A further prophecy, of Merlin (but clearly not one of Geoffrey's) is mentioned in Book ii.1, in a curious episode: a woman cited Merlin's prophecy that a king in his position would die if he walked across *Llech Lafar*, 'The Talking Stone'. Henry, Gerald said, was aware of the prophecy and deliberately walked across the stone, proclaimed Merlin a liar, but was ultimately discomfited. Gerald, as is so often the case, was our only authority for this 'traditional' material, which is not to say that he invented it.

Other, related, prophetic material can be used both to show how popular the Merlin material was and to confirm its links with British tradition. Among the rather free-floating, political proph-ecies in Latin found in manuscripts, particularly of the fourteenth century, we find those known either as *Prophetiae Merlini Silvestris*, or 'Prophecies of the Eagle'. These sometimes accompany versions of Geoffrey's *Historia Regum Britanniae*. They echo those of Geoffrey in style but not in content, and are closely related to much of the prophetic material ascribed both to Merlin Silvester and to the Irish St Moling by Gerald of Wales. Several Welsh translations of this material exist, one inserted into the middle of the Cotton Cleopatra B.v version of *Brut y Brenhinedd*, the translation into Welsh of Geoffrey's *Historia*, at the point at which Geoffrey refers to a prophetic eagle at Shaftesbury. We should note that at this point Geoffrey claimed to disbelieve the eagle and therefore refused to reproduce the prophecies (Bk ii.9). Further on in *Historia Regum Britanniae*, Alanus of Brittany tested the authority of the Angelic Voice's command by comparing it with 'Prophecies of the Eagle' at Shaftesbury as well as with prophecies of the Sibyl and Merlin (Bk xii.18). Presumably, then, Geoffrey was referring, if not to existing material, at least to an existing notion of a prophetic eagle, whether connected to Shaftesbury or not. However, in the absence of published editions of this material, not to speak of full studies, it is difficult to establish the relationship between Gerald's Merlin Silvester prophecies, the probably later Latin and Welsh versions and an earlier Welsh tradition. It is difficult not to suspect that Gerald might have been instrumental in inventing or at least adapting some of these, given that he attributed some to Merlin and some to Moling, which should arguably have come from two quite different sources, and given that at least one of Gerald's prophecies that mentioned Ireland in the Welsh versions specified Brittany instead. Gerald is perhaps not so very different from Geoffrey in this matter.

As we have seen above, Gerald of Wales differentiated between two Merlins. In his *Itinerarium Kambrie*, Book ii.8, Gerald stated that the first, Merlin Ambrosius, was associated with Vortigern and Carmarthen; the second, Merlin Silvester or Celidonius, was associated with Scotland and had become a visionary as a result of battle, fleeing to the wilderness. Gerald pointedly located this second Merlin in the Arthurian period. Here, Gerald was trying to make sense of what is often considered a confusion in Geoffrey's writings. Gerald's Merlin Ambrosius was the Merlin of *Prophetiae Merlini* and *Historia Regum Britanniae*; his prophecies were, as Gerald noted (*Expugnatio Hibernica*, preface to Bk iii), well known. The other Merlin, the one Gerald hoped to rescue from the obscurity of oral British bardic tradition by publishing his *Liber Vaticinorum*, corresponded to another Merlin, with different biographical details, appearing in Geoffrey's later work, *Vita*

Merlini. At least one of the triads ('Three Skilful Bards were at Arthur's Court', no. 87) followed Gerald's differentiation, as did several medieval Welsh poets. Although Geoffrey insisted that the Merlin(s) in his two texts were the same, the clear differences in their stories have provoked much discussion, from Gerald to the present day. As usual, much of this discussion concerns the extent to which Geoffrey invented material or adapted existing 'tradition' and to what extent we might be able to recover earlier 'tradition' that exists only in Geoffrey's work or other texts heavily influenced by Geoffrey. This brings us to the *Vita Merlini*.

In his *Life of Merlin* (*Vita Merlini*), composed probably between 1148 and 1151, Geoffrey presented what to us seems to be quite a different Merlin from that of *Historia Regum Britanniae*. Geoffrey, however, presented this Merlin as the same as that of the *Historia*, and glossed over Merlin's now extremely long life span, from the period of Vortigern (as in *Historia Regum Britanniae*) in the presumed mid-fifth century to the time of the battle of Arfderydd (which can be taken as the unnamed battle at the beginning of *Vita Merlini*), occurring according to *Annales Cambriae* in 573. 'Many years and many kings had come and gone' (l. 19) said Geoffrey, by way of introduction to the events of the *Vita*. Geoffrey then related how Merlin went to battle at an unnamed place with Peredurus (Peredur – the Welsh equivalents are here given in brackets) and Rodarcus (Rhydderch), rulers of north Wales and Cumbria respectively, against Guennolous (Gwenddolau), ruler of Scotland. Merlin's side won the day but the brutality of battle proved too much for Merlin's sensibilities and he was overcome by madness. He lived in the wilderness but was sought by his sister, Ganieda (Gwenddydd), Rodarcus's wife, as well as by Guendoloena, Merlin's wife. The invocation of these, as well as some music, brought Merlin back to his senses and he returned to Rodarcus's court, although once there his madness returned and he decided to return to his wilderness in the Calidon woods. There was a slight delay as Merlin claimed that Rodarcus's wife was unfaithful to him, and as she tested Merlin's powers of divination she tricked him, apparently, into foretelling three different deaths for the same person. This prophecy was fulfilled as the person in question died a 'three-fold' death. Here also,

Merlin referred to events of *Historia Regum Britanniae*, specifically Aurelius Conanus's murder of his uncle Constantinus (Bk xi.5). Merlin returned to Rodarcus's court for his former wife's wedding (who had, meanwhile, given up on him and was preparing to remarry), killed the bridegroom and was forced, against his will, to remain at court.

After his return to court, Merlin produced his first extended political prophecy (ll. 580–688). This prophecy is based partly on events in *Historia Regum Britanniae*, partly on events to do with northern Wales and the northern British and Scottish kingdoms, and partly on events between the establishment of the Anglo-Saxon kingdoms to the civil war between Stephen and Matilda. Merlin ended by stating that this was what he explained to Vortigern, a clear connection to the Merlin of *Historia Regum Britanniae* and *Prophetiae Merlini*. Then Telegesinus (Taliesin) was introduced as having come recently from Brittany where he was visiting Gildas. Rodarcus was discovered to have died and Telegesinus met with Merlin. Telegesinus explained many natural phenomena to Merlin and described British and European geography to him. This included several fantastical places, including the *Insula Pomorum*, 'The Island of Apples', which was a paradisiacal island ruled by nine sisters, including one named Morgen, a healer. Telegesinus specifically stated that Arthur was taken by 'us' (himself, Morgen and her sisters, presumably) after the battle of *Camblanus*. Merlin noted that Britain was in a dire state, whereupon Telegesinus urged Arthur's recall. Merlin rejected this plan, however, and gave his second significant political prophecy: Britain, he says, was fated to live under the invader's rule for a long period of time, until the return of Conanus from Brittany, along with Cadualadrus. Merlin described this return in terms similar to those of *Armes Prydein* (ll. 959–75), concluding that the time of Brutus would be restored. Merlin went on to describe for Telegesinus (who had, of course, been in Brittany and had missed all this) the invitation of the Saxons under Vortigern, and the events following it, more or less as related in *Historia Regum Britanniae*. Merlin and Telegesinus visited a new spring, and Merlin was once again rendered sane. Telegesinus continued with his exposition of geography and natural history.

They were joined by visitors from Rodarcus's court, and Merlin favoured these with a description of birds and their behaviour. A second madman, Maeldinus, appeared; his name was derived from that of the legendary medieval Irish voyager, Mael Dúin, although it isn't clear why. Merlin disclosed that this was one of his companions who, along with others, ate magical apples and was rendered mad; the apples, Merlin revealed, were intended to derange him, left for him by a woman he had spurned. The water of the spring cured the man, who became a companion to Merlin. The life finishes with its third major prophecy, from Ganieda, who had joined them in the woods, touching on events of the civil war, but also referring to fighting among the Welsh and famine. She concluded by warning the Normans to depart as Britain no longer had anything to offer them. Merlin rejoiced that the prophetic gift had apparently passed from him to her, and the text ended by identifying its author, Geoffrey 'of Monmouth', as the author of *Historia Regum Britanniae* as well.

The question is, what did Geoffrey adapt, and what did he invent? Geoffrey did not invent the name and general role of Telgesinus/Taliesin; neither did he invent the names, nor some of the aspects, of Peredurus/Peredur, Guennolous/Gwenddolau, Ganieda/Gwenddydd and Rodarcus/Rhydderch (whose epithet in Welsh tradition, *hael*, 'generous' is echoed in Geoffrey's description of him as *largus* in line 730). Morgen's origins are not certain. Guendoloena and Maeldinus are characters without antecedents in Welsh tradition, although their names are not without precedent: Guendoloena would seem to be a female version of Gwenddolau, and Maeldinus as noted above is the name of a well-known Irish character, albeit one whose role in *Vita Merlini* has no logical explanation. Geoffrey did not invent a prophetic Myrddin, either, but his creation of Merlin almost certainly placed a much greater significance on this figure than he previously enjoyed, as was the case with Arthur.

Unlike *Historia Regum Britanniae* and *Prophetiae Merlini*, *Vita Merlini* was not widely copied. It exists today only in twelve manuscripts: one full version and several incomplete. Its earliest manuscript (York Minster, MS XVI.Q.14, *c.*1200) is now incomplete, but perhaps only lost its ending relatively late in its history. Merlin of the *Vita* remained a marginal character. The usual scholarly assumption has been that Geoffrey drew on, in part, a body of Welsh prophetic material associated with a figure who descended into madness after traumatic experience in battle, one with analogues in other Celtic traditions. But why did Geoffrey only produce this version of Merlin so long after he had presented quite a different Merlin, named Emrys, in *Historia Regum Britanniae*? The accepted, if not entirely satisfying, explanation has usually been that Geoffrey had only a partial knowledge of this figure until the later part of his life. There is, however, a different explanation, one that does not throw up so many implausibilities (why would Geoffrey correct himself? Where would he find the 'correct' version?) and which stresses Geoffrey's active role in acquiring, and manipulating, 'traditional' material.

We have seen that medieval Welsh literature included a significant tradition of prophetic poetry, which we have discussed already with respect to *Armes Prydein* and Cynan and Cadwaladr. This poetry was sometimes anonymous, and sometimes associated with named figures. Some are vague in their referencing. Some, like *Armes Prydein*, are so specific in their referencing and so precise in their demands for future action that they are more political statements than prophecies. Some prophecy is attributed to historic figures who composed praise poetry to rulers, such as the sixth-century poet Taliesin (though this tends to occur in late poems) and our somewhat obscure Myrddin.

Myrddin was clearly a figure of importance before Geoffrey's time. The very early Welsh poem, *Y Gododdin*, which contains what might be the earliest reference to Arthur, also contains what might or might not be the earliest reference to a figure named Myrddin: line 466 refers to *gwenwawt mirdyn*, 'the fair song (?) of Myrddin'. Needless to say, all the caveats applied to the mention of Arthur in this poem (uncertain date, uncertain historicity, possible ease of interpolation) apply also to the reference to Myrddin. Another reference to Myrddin in Welsh poetry is found in *Armes Prydein*. The second stanza is introduced with *Dysgogan Myrdin*, 'Myrddin foretells it' (l. 17). It is, of course, possible that the name Myrddin was introduced by the scribe of the Book of Taliesin later than the poem's composition, replacing another name.

Obviously, Geoffrey adopted the name of this figure, Myrddin, for his Merlin, with a sound change to avoid recalling the French word *merde*, with its unattractive associations. The story of this Welsh Myrddin, however, cannot be clearly established; it would seem to be the story of the Merlin of *Vita Merlini*, hence the argument that Geoffrey, having made the prophetic Emrys of Welsh tradition into Merlin for *Historia Regum Britanniae*, later 'corrected' himself, giving the 'true' version that appeared in *Vita Merlini*. There are six poems that have long been considered to preserve, in fragmentary fashion, a native Welsh, pre-Galfredian story and prophecies of a northern British, prophetic, madman figure associated with the court of Rhydderch Hael, Gwenddydd, Gwenddolau and, in particular, the battle of Arfderydd (all of which show up in *Vita Merlini*, if we take the unnamed battle causing all the problems to be Arfderydd). Two of these poems, *Gwasgargerdd Fyrddin yn y Bedd*, 'The Separation-Song of Myrddin in the Grave', and *Peirian Faban*, 'Commanding Youth', are not thought to be early enough in date to represent potentially a pre-Geoffrey tradition, although the former is, as noted above, of interest in that it contains material similar to one of the prophecies attributed by Gerald of Wales to Merlin Silvester. The two earliest poems containing the greatest amount of biographical information (such as it is), *Afallennau*, 'Apple-Tree verses', and *Oianau* '"O Piglet" verses', are found in the Black Book of Carmarthen, a mid-thirteenth-century manuscript. They suggest a prophet wandering among the trees in the wood of Celidon, partly addressing pigs, who was responsible for the death of several of his sister Gwenddydd's children, and whose lord Gwenddolau had fallen at the battle of Arfderydd (Arthuret, near Carlisle). Rhydderch Hael, king of Strathclyde in the late sixth century (mentioned in Adomnán's *Life of St Columba*) appears as an object of fear. The problem is, these poems had no author cited, and Myrddin was not mentioned in them. Later, post-Geoffrey, material seems to have made this connection: we cannot rule out the possibility that this was done on the basis of what Geoffrey himself said about Merlin.

The earliest poem to connect Myrddin with Arfderydd, keeping in mind our difficulty in dating medieval Welsh poems, is also found in the Black Book of Carmarthen: *Ymddiddan Myrddin a Thaliesin*, 'The Colloquy of Merlin and Taliesin'. As in *Vita Merlini*, Taliesin, full of knowledge, spoke with Myrddin, who had a prophetic gift. Divided into two halves, its first part concerned a battle between Gwynedd and Dyfed and mentioned in particular Maelgwn, ruler of Gwynedd in the sixth century. Taliesin appeared to speak of the Gwynedd material, Myrddin of the Dyfed material. The second half of the poem concerned the battle of Arfderydd, which is not surprising as it was well attested in medieval Welsh literary tradition, being mentioned in several triads and associated most often with Gwenddolau. The poem also mentioned Celidon Wood and madness, although it did not directly associate Myrddin with any of this.

A further poem, found in the Red Book of Hergest as well as in another medieval manuscript (although there lacking its first part), specifically associated Myrddin with Gwenddolau, Rhydderch and Arfderydd: *Cyfoesi Myrddin a Gwenddydd ei Chwaer*, 'The Prophecy of Myrddin and Gwenddydd his Sister'. It specified that its author was driven mad because of Gwenddolau's death in the battle and referred to wild men. Depending on one's view of its date, it either represented an earlier tradition that Geoffrey drew upon, or was the product of Geoffrey's adaptations and inventions. In the *Cyfoesi*, Myrddin did not seem to have been afraid of Rhydderch and was on good terms with his sister – this is in keeping with the Merlin of *Vita Merlini* but contradicts the situation of the unnamed persona of the earliest poems, *Afallennau* and *Oianau*. *Cyfoesi Myrddin a Gwenddydd* also gave one crucial clue: Gwenddydd repeatedly referred to Myrddin as *Llallogan*. Latin materials from northern Britain concerning St Kentigern spoke, in fragmentary fashion, of a prophetic wildman named Lailoken, associated with King Rederech (Rhydderch) and a three-fold death (which was not mentioned in the Welsh poetry at issue here); some of these specifically equated Lailoken with Merlin (not Myrddin) and several occur only once, grouped together in a fifteenth-century manuscript also containing Geoffrey's *Vita Merlini*. Arfderydd was not mentioned in any of these texts, but in one Lailoken was said to have lost his reason at a battle on a plain 'between Lidel and Carwannok', which is plausibly near Arthuret (Arfderydd).

The Lailoken material surely originated in the same tradition that provided Merlin or Myrddin with a northern profile and a particular biography. It was long assumed that when the northern British prophetic wildman figure became known in south Wales he took on the name Myrddin and a location at Carmarthen through a spurious etymologizing of the name for Carmarthen. Caerfyrddin was originally derived from Moridunum, the Roman name of the town ('sea fortress'), but *caer* ('fortress') was added (in a tautological formation) and then the whole reinterpreted as *caer* + personal name Myrddin. This, it has usually been assumed, was before Geoffrey's time. According to this scheme of things, Geoffrey's role was relatively passive: he included an existing Carmarthen Myrddin in *Historia Regum Britanniae*, although he attributed to him extra material, that is, the episode of the dragons (itself originally located in north Wales); then, at a later date in *Vita Merlini* he expanded the story of the northern Lailoken, which he had either not known previously or had omitted. Thus, in this view, Geoffrey made use of an already combined Myrddin/Lailoken in both his works, but in the later text restored this composite figure to his 'proper' 'Lailoken', 'northern' role in Welsh tradition. That Geoffrey portrayed two Merlins is not in question: what has been asked recently, by Oliver Padel, is why we should assume that Geoffrey was at pains to rectify a mistake or omission in his source material rather than that, as was certainly the case elsewhere, he took an active role in reinventing his material? What if Geoffrey himself merged several disparate strands of material (as he was wont to do): the prophetic poetry specifically attributed to Myrddin; the Latin Lailoken material; the Welsh poetry which perhaps concerned a Lailoken-like figure associated with the battle of Arfderydd, but not yet identified with Myrddin? It is highly suggestive in this context that Geoffrey was made bishop-elect of St Asaph, a new diocese in north Wales centred on an early Christian site that, according to its earliest records, was founded by St Kentigern and whose primary dedication was to that saint. These 'earliest' records of St Asaph, however, post-date Geoffrey: the claim that Kentigern founded St Asaph appears first in Jocelin of Furness's *Life of St Kentigern,* written *c.*1180; the earliest evidence we have that this story was known at St Asaph is a charter in the *Llyfr Coch Asaph.* This manuscript was collated in the fourteenth century, and it refers to a charter supposedly discovered in 1256, but the charter's language and form suggest a twelfth-century date. The very name of the diocese first appeared in connection with Geoffrey's appointment to it; it seems strongly possible that he was responsible for making the connection between St Asaph and Kentigern. The difficulty, and it is not inconsiderable, is that it is by no means certain that Geoffrey had much to do with St Asaph during or even after the time of writing *Vita Merlini* in which the Kentigern material figured.

We should perhaps note that the Latin and Welsh versions of the biography of Gruffydd ap Cynan, with their origins in the second half of the twelfth century, quoted a prophecy that also appeared in a poem, *Dygogan Awen,* in the Book of Taliesin which clearly belonged to the relatively shadowy prophetic Taliesin figure; these texts attribute it to Merlinus (*Vita Griffini filii Conani,* ch. 8) or Merdin (*Historia Gruffud vab Kenan*) – not, we should note, Myrddin. It is difficult to be certain, but the biography would seem to be quoting it from the poem, not the other way around – if so, this is an example of 'traditional' prophetic material whose attribution has changed, and changed to Geoffrey's version, not to a 'traditional' Welsh version, at least in terms of the name of the character. Unfortunately, the fact that the earliest manuscript of *Historia Gruffudd vab Kenan* dates from the later thirteenth century makes it impossible to say whether or not the striking use of the Latin form of the name was that of the original adaptation.

The Merlin of *Historia Regum Britanniae* and *Prophetiae Merlini* was overwhelmingly popular, in contrast to the Merlin of *Vita Merlini.* Merlin's later literary offshoots, particularly in an Arthurian context, originated in Merlin 'Ambrosius', not in Merlin 'Silvester'. The limited influence of Geoffrey's later Merlin might be seen to support the assumption that the combining of these prophetic figures was a pre-Geoffrey development: it is tempting to argue that Geoffrey's invention was of more interest than his more traditional rendering of the same character. The apparent Celticity of the wildman Lailoken story – there is a relatively detailed Irish counterpart, that of the tale of *Suibne Geilt* – could also be cited in support of a Welsh Myrddin, one relatively untouched by Geoffrey. This sort of argument, however, assumes that Geoffrey's contribution was that of an outsider, both in terms of collecting and use of sources, and in terms of later influence. This view of Geoffrey is not supported by the evidence.

9

Welsh Tradition and Geoffrey's Legacy

Geoffrey can reasonably be seen as an intellectual understandable in the context of Norman rule. His life at Oxford, his simplistic portrait of a supposed translation of native, vernacular sources, his governance in absentia of a Welsh diocese, all conspire to make him seem a very Anglo-Norman figure, isolated from Wales. It is important not to treat Geoffrey in such isolation. Clearly, he had strong links to both the sources and the thematic preoccupations of Welsh historical tradition. Geoffrey's changes to his source material were themselves adopted subsequently back into Welsh tradition – sometimes in contradiction of their original nature. Geoffrey is best understood as Cambro-Norman, with a foot in both traditions.

When we consider Geoffrey's intervention in Welsh tradition, the example of Modred/Medraut proves particularly striking. Medraut appeared in *Annales Cambriae* as someone who fell at the same time as Arthur; the later medieval Welsh poets seemed to include him among the heroic figures of the past to whom they alluded. He was also included in complimentary terms as one of the 'Twenty-Four Knights of Arthur's Court' in a text whose earliest written version dated from the fifteenth century but probably contained older material. Yet, in keeping with his role as a villain in *Historia Regum Britanniae*, he was presented as an evil-doer in the four medieval triads in which he appears. One of these, 'Three Men of Shame were in the Island of Britain' (no. 51), was drawn entirely from translations of Geoffrey and retold his version of Arthur's fall; another, 'Three Sinister Hand Slaps of the Island of Britain' (no. 53), mentioned Medraut only in a late version (Peniarth 50); another, 'Three Violent Ravagings of the Island of Britain' (no. 54), seemed to refer to a competition between Arthur and Medraut and a blow to Gwenhwyfar, Arthur's wife, and the final one, 'Three Unfortunate Counsels of the Island of Britain' (no. 59), referred solely to events at Camlan. Medraut was also referred to by the fifteenth-century poet Tudur Aled as involved in 'treachery'. The later medieval Arthurian tale, *Breudwyt Ronabwy*, 'The Dream of Rhonabwy', also mentioned Medraut as Arthur's opponent at Camlan. While there may have been a pre-Geoffrey story about Medraut and Gwenhwyfar (perhaps influenced by or parallel to the story of Gwenhwyfar's abduction by Melwas as related by Caradog of Llancarfan in his *Vita Gildae*, 'The Life of St Gildas', dated to the twelfth century), it is a safe inference that the final version of the story in which Modred betrayed Arthur was mainly due to Geoffrey's influence.

The main avenue of influence by Geoffrey on Welsh-language historical material was, not surprisingly, the translation (using the term in its broadest sense) of *Historia Regum Britanniae* into Welsh. Welsh antiquarian writers once thought these were the 'ancient book in the British language' that Geoffrey referred to as his source, but they were in fact translations of the *Historia* into Welsh. These are variously titled, but the commonest title is *Brut y Brenhinedd* (plural *Brutiau*). The Welsh translations survive in some sixty manuscripts, with the earliest versions stemming from three main groups originating in the early thirteenth century. The earliest translations followed Geoffrey's text relatively faithfully, trans-lating characters' names into their already established Welsh forms (very often into their Welsh 'originals') where they had them, often bringing their orthography up to date or finding close equivalents; where it was not possible to find exact equivalents, they Cambricized Geoffrey's forms. Later versions of the fourteenth and fifteenth centuries varied considerably, in particular adding much more material.

Material was added, usually from Welsh sources: the tale *Cyfranc Lludd a Llefelys*, mentioned above, is one example; the 'Prophecies of the Eagle' is another. One group of manuscripts, represented by National Library of Wales Peniarth 21, added material from conti-nental romances, Wace, Layamon and others – many of these, of course, themselves were translations of Geoffrey's *Historia Regum Britanniae* into other vernacular languages. The Welsh translations also led directly to the keeping of a Latin chronicle (now lost), conceived as a continuation of Geoffrey's history and hence bearing the name, in its Welsh translations, of *Brut y Tywysogion*. This Welsh text is often found in the same manuscripts as *Brut y Brenhinedd* – one manuscript (British Library MS Cotton Cleopatra B.v) directly states the connection in its opening lines. Also often found in these manuscripts is a Welsh version of the Latin *Historia Daretis Phrygii de excidio Troiae* (in Welsh, *Ystoria Daret*), filling in the story of Troy as a prelude to Geoffrey's own account of the Trojan foundation of Britain.

Of the continental translators, Wace stood out as having added many of the features we now associate so strongly with the Arthurian story. His *Roman de Brut*, completed in 1155, recast Geoffrey's scheme so that the Arthurian section occupied about one-third rather than Geoffrey's one-fifth of the whole, and included the first account of the round table, specifying that the *Bretun*, arguably the 'Bretons' not the 'British', told stories about it. This reminds us, once again, that Brittany had its own, often closely related, pool of pseudo-historical and Arthurian material upon which Geoffrey may well have drawn. Such was the popularity of Wace's version of Geoffrey's history that the name Brutus spawned a word in Welsh, *brut*, signifying 'history', a use paralleled in English, although not appearing as frequently.

Wace's was the most influential of all the revisions and vernacular versions of Geoffrey's *Historia*. Nevertheless, we might mention Layamon's *Brut*, the first rendering of Geoffrey, mainly via Wace, into Middle English; although its influence was limited, its vision of history made an interesting comparison with Geoffrey's. Probably composed in the last decades of the twelfth century and claiming to rely on both Wace and Bede for its material, the poem in fact abandoned Bede early on to concentrate on the material found in Wace. Layamon took advantage of the ambiguities of Geoffrey's ending (the obscure fate of Arthur, the apparent endorsement, ultimately, of the English rule) to recast it as a history of the English in which he retained a sense of English continuity and avoided passing to the contemporary English the stain of the wrongdoings of the Anglo-Saxon invaders. Crucially, in a few lines Arthur went from being the figure whose return the 'Britons' (*Bruttes*) awaited to being the hope of the 'English people' (*Anglen*) (*Brut*, ll. 14,292–7). Like Geoffrey, and unlike Wace, Layamon was concerned mainly with the overall scheme of history rather than with individual episodes, as important as some of these episodes might have been. Also like Geoffrey, and unlike Wace, Layamon was dismissive, rather than overtly critical, of the Welsh. The influence of Layamon's *Brut* on English historiography, however, is thought to have been minimal: the various different prose *Bruts* that followed owed more to elaborations of Wace and other texts than to Layamon's poem, despite its seminal position in English Arthurian studies.

Despite the scepticism it aroused in some of his contemporaries as to its accuracy, Geoffrey's vision of British history had an overwhelming influence on English historiographical tradition. One of the earliest sceptics was Ranulf Higden (d.1364), who dutifully noted in his *Polychronicon* several occasions on which Geoffrey's version contradicted that of other sources. He refused to include the story of Merlin and was clearly of two minds about Arthur, on the one hand being suspicious that he was not mentioned in histories apart from British or English ones, and on the other hand satisfying himself by commenting that every nation provides accounts of its own heroes, whose purpose might be literary rather than historical. Nevertheless, much of Geoffrey's material was included by him, unquestioned. The most significant challenge to Geoffrey's story came from the Italian historian Polydore Vergil in his *Anglica Historia* (1534). Henry VIII's antiquary, John Leland, bravely attempted to rescue Arthur from Polydore's attack, with limited success. Nevertheless, Geoffrey's account remained a significant influence on English historical thought, albeit often indirectly. In Wales, the Tudor official Sir John Pryse wrote his *Historiae Britannicae Defensio* (published posthumously in 1573) to refute Polydore, although he agreed with him in many particulars. For the most part, Geoffrey's version prevailed in Wales, sometimes controversially, into the nineteenth century, finding continued support in such vivid writers as Elis Gruffydd (*c*.1490–*c*.1552), Theophilus Evans (1693–1767) and the antiquary Edward Williams (Iolo Morganwg, 1747–1826). Not until the publication of *Hanes y Brytaniaid a'r Cymry* by Robert John Pryse ('Gweirydd ap Rhys') in 1872–4 was the tide decisively turned against Geoffrey. One interesting, if minor, footnote to the strength of this Galfredian, Arthurian view of the British was the adaptation, by a Welsh writer in the fifteenth century, of a story well known from English sources (based ultimately on a continental original). This story concerned holy oil presented to Thomas Becket by the Virgin Mary, which was intended to be used to anoint rightful kings of England and was accompanied by a prophecy concerning their nature. The Welsh version, *Darogan yr Olew Bendigaid*, 'The Prophecy of the Blessed Oil', gave the holy oil an Arthurian prehistory: it was said to be the same oil that was used by Dubricius to anoint Arthur in *Historia Regum Britanniae*. The kings of the English in the Becket episode were turned in this Welsh work into 'kings of this island' (i.e. Britain). Clearly, the idea of regaining Ynys Prydein, in particular in Geoffrey's Arthurian-dominated version, retained its power even in entirely different circumstances.

The overall context for all Welsh prophetic literature was the promise of the recovery of British (Welsh) political sovereignty, as symbolized by the red dragon of *Historia Brittonum*. From about 1200 onwards, the amount of Welsh prophetic poetry in particular speaking of deliverance from the English increased; the number of named deliverers was augmented as well. One of the more interesting aspects of this prophetic tradition, as noted above, is Arthur's absence from the list of named deliverers. Cynan and Cadwaladr dominated the earliest material, including that which was later understood as the 'Myrddin' material, whether or not it mentioned Myrddin. In the thirteenth and fourteenth centuries, the period in which Wales finally, and decisively, lost its political independence from England, several figures, often of ambiguous identification, dominated the literature of prophecy, including Beli, Llywelyn and, above all, Owain. The latter was identified either as Owain ap Thomas ap Rhodri, also known as Owain Lawgoch or Yvain de Galles, the last direct heir of the Gwynedd dynasty who was assassinated in France in 1378. Another 'redeemer Owain' was found in Owain Glyndŵr.

The relatively ambiguous prophetic material became more and more politically pointed, reaching its apogee in the *cywydd brud*, 'prophetic verse', in the Wars of the Roses. There was a subtle shift in emphasis: although freedom from bondage was still the general wish, the fulfilment of the prophecies was becoming an end in itself. Specific political events became more prominent and the seizing of the throne of England by a particular person (the redeemer, or *mab darogan*, 'son of prophecy') was envisaged, with poets plumping for both Yorkist and Lancastrian candidates depending on their connection with Wales. We should note that Arthurian and Merlin's prophetic associations were deployed by English propagandists for both sides as well, although for different reasons. The accession of the 'Welsh' Henry Tudor to the English throne was widely held to represent the longed-for fulfilment of these Welsh prophecies.

Geoffrey's Arthur did not insert himself in the list of Welsh heroes who were to represent the success of the red dragon foretold so long ago by Ambrosius or Emrys. This would suggest that, despite the hints noted above that Geoffrey did not invent Arthur's ambiguous end or return, he was not linked to the idea of a redeemer figure as such (and we should note that while he is an important part of the prophetic oil's prehistory in *Darogan yr Olew Bendigaid*, it is not implied that he will return). We should also remember that Geoffrey's prophetic material, when it cited redeemer figures by name, included Cynan and Cadwaladr but not Arthur. Geoffrey's British hero Arthur would be taken over as a national redeemer mainly by English tradition.

It is somewhat ironic, given the relative weakness of Geoffrey's influence on the Welsh prophetic tradition at least as regards Arthur that there is considerable debate about Geoffrey's influence on the prophetic poetry in quite a different respect, one that has nothing to do with Arthur. Geoffrey has been credited with introducing the idea of using animal symbolism to indicate particular people in the Welsh (and non-Welsh) prophetic material. It isn't clear to what extent Geoffrey was the originator of this literary technique: it occurs in the Old and New Testaments (Daniel, ch. 7 and ch. 8, and

Revelation especially). Pre-Geoffrey Welsh sources included strikingly few examples, the most notable being from *Armes Prydein* in which Cynan and Cadwaladr are *deu arth*, 'two bears'. Two different genres show the use of animal imagery much more commonly: these are 'heroic' poetry and the lists of names preserved in genealogical collections. Gildas's *De Excidio Britanniae*, one of Geoffrey's sources, also notably used animal imagery in describing contemporary British rulers. Finally, the dragons of the Vortigern story clearly exemplified animal symbolism in a prophetic context. Yet, for all this, pre-Geoffrey Welsh prophetic poetry as such did not use this technique and its increasing popularity in post-Geoffrey Welsh prophetic poetry has, although not uncontroversially, been seen as the result of influence from Geoffrey and from English prophetic poetry.

Geoffrey's influence on Welsh literary and historical tradition was considerable. It is also clear that Geoffrey, at least in *Historia Regum Britanniae*, followed the notable themes in the earlier traditions quite faithfully. One question, probably unanswerable, concerns the extent to which Geoffrey had direct access to Welsh-language materials: did he speak or read Welsh? If not, did he have some sort of translator? While the obscurities surrounding Geoffrey's life, and those surrounding the use of the various languages at issue during Geoffrey's lifetime in what might have been his place of origin are profound, nevertheless it is surprising how little the question of Geoffrey's linguistic abilities has been explored. He referred to Latin as *lingua nostra* (Bk ii.1): this does not at all rule out a knowledge, even a profound knowledge, of Welsh, given the complicated linguistic situation of Norman Britain. No one would suggest that he was a native English speaker, but he frequently showed a lively and informed interest in English words and, above all, place-names. Geoffrey's spellings suggested that his was a knowledge of the spoken rather than the written language, a knowledge that could have been gained at Oxford. His knowledge of Welsh was equally well illustrated in place-names. He invented, for example, a Cambro-Latin version of the English place-name Shaftesbury, *Mons Paladur*: the Latin *mons* presumably translated what Geoffrey took to be *beorg*, 'hill', rather than the correct *burh*, 'fortified town'; the less common Welsh word *paladur* correctly translated 'shaft' (Bk ii.9). Geoffrey's comment that the Trojan language was known as *curuum Graecum*, 'crooked Greek', before coming to be known, after Brutus, as 'British' (Bk i.16) almost certainly referred to an invented and deliberately fanciful etymology for the Welsh word for the Welsh language, *Cymraeg*, by linking it to the Britons' purported classical origins. Geoffrey, or perhaps a predecessor, almost certainly presented *Cymraeg* as having the constituent elements *Cam Roeg*, 'crooked Greek' (the asterisk denotes a form that is assumed but not attested). The point is that the phrase *curuum Graecum* would make no sense unless the audience knew what the Latin phrase would be in Welsh, and furthermore knew that *Groeg*, 'Greek', could lose its initial 'G' under these circumstances. The fact that Geoffrey did not provide an explanation is surely significant. Some years later, Gerald of Wales repeated the claim, but with a laborious explanation (*Descriptio Kambriae*, i.7), which suggests that the phrase was not well known, and which underlines the fact that Gerald needed to explain it to his Norman audience. Geoffrey, on the other hand, either was so familiar with the issues at hand that he forgot to explain the pun to his audience, or intended it for a small, Welsh-speaking part of his audience.

Geoffrey's knowledge of Welsh would seem to have been oral rather than written, judging from his usual, Latinate spellings of place-names. It is also notable, in the light of claims made for a Breton connection for Geoffrey, that Geoffrey's place-names show no sign of being of Breton, rather than Welsh, spelling, the two of course being closely linked. Geoffrey's Latinizations of Welsh names, such as Taliesin to Telgesinus, are philologically impressive. It is useful in this context to compare the attitude of Gerald of Wales. Of Cambro-Norman background, Gerald was sympathetic to the Welsh language, quoted it at times although not at length, compared Welsh words to Latin and Greek words, commented on the relationship of Welsh to Cornish and Breton, explained puns and jokes, and in the introduction to his uncompleted or unpublished book of prophecy, purported to translate from the Welsh, albeit with help. He knew enough to interpret the pun about 'crooked Greek' that Geoffrey had neglected to explain. However, Gerald's main source for Welsh historical tradition was Geoffrey of Monmouth's *Historia* – he cited its material, uncredited, with approval. However, when Gerald referred to Geoffrey by name, he was vehemently critical: Gerald related with some relish the tale of Meilyr the prophet, who could be rid of harassing demons by having a copy of St John's Gospel placed on his lap; if it were replaced by Geoffrey's *Historia*, the demons would return in force, and stay for longer than usual (*Itinerarium Kambriae*, i.5).

Conclusion

Geoffrey's keen advocacy of the concept of a heroic and civilized British history set him apart from his contemporaries. Geoffrey wrote soon before 1139, in the very early stages of a civil war that was to last until 1154. The *Historia Regum Britanniae* is, to a certain extent, about the dangers of disunity, a strong current in medieval Welsh writing elsewhere, as we have seen above and one needing no explanation in the context of the Norman civil war of Geoffrey's time. Geoffrey depicted attempts at empire-building among the Britons that arguably could be seen as offering a model for the ambitious Normans, but his celebration of the British identity and its ancient dignity was contrary to what contemporary writers such as Henry of Huntingdon and William of Malmesbury were presenting as a vision of the British.

It was of central importance to Geoffrey that his tale be told in a suitably 'historical' fashion, without gaps and with properly believable characters and events. Instead of a disconnected and disinterested journey through the antiquities of Britain, he sought to adapt the more sustained narratives of Gildas, the *Historia Brittonum* and the overarching narratives of Celtic synthetic history that located their local histories imaginatively within the mainstream of Classical, Biblical and European history. His narrative had the most enduring influence of all histories of Britain. The chief beneficiary of all this, arguably, was Arthur, who remains Geoffrey's enduring legacy. Geoffrey took the Arthur of *Historia Brittonum* and placed him among a host of historically respectable figures, some such as Maxen and Carausius, who were secure in their historicity, albeit in the process of acquiring legendary accretions. As a literary and historical figure, Arthur was profoundly important, in Welsh as much as in European tradition. Geoffrey's passion for the chronological march of political history, however, meant that Arthur was, for him, only one of the many British kings that he celebrated.

Select Bibliography

A full bibliography of Geoffrey of Monmouth would occupy a volume on its own. I have restricted the selections here to basic texts, to a limited number of standard secondary sources and to recent works of particular note. Particular attention has been paid to areas not as well represented in other discussions of Geoffrey's work.

Introduction

Curley, Michael J., *Geoffrey of Monmouth*. Twayne's English Authors Series (New York: Twayne Publishers, 1994).

Griscom, Achom (ed.), *The Historia Regum Britanniae of Geoffrey of Monmouth. With contributions to the study of its place in early British history. Together with a literal translation of the Welsh manuscript no. LXI of Jesus College Oxford by Robert Ellis Jones* (London and New York: Longmans & Co., 1929).

Hughes, Kathleen, 'British Museum MS. Cotton Vespasian A.xiv (*Vitae Sanctorum Wallensium*): its Purpose and Provenance', in N. K. Chadwick, et al. (eds), *Studies in the Early British Church* (Cambridge: Cambridge University Press, 1958), pp. 183–200.

Reeve, Michael D. and Neil Wright (ed. and trans.), *Geoffrey of Monmouth. The History of the Kings of Britain* (Woodbridge: The Boydell Press, 2007).

Tatlock, J. S. P., *The Legendary History of Britain. Geoffrey of Monmouth's Historia Regum Britanniae and its Early Vernacular Versions* (Berkeley and Los Angeles, California: University of California Press, 1950).

Thorpe, Lewis (trans.), *Geoffrey of Monmouth. The History of the Kings of Britain* (Harmondsworth: Penguin, 1966).

1 Geoffrey of Monmouth and his work

Davies, R. R., *The Age of Conquest. Wales 1063–1415* (Oxford: Oxford University Press, 1991).

Gillingham, John, *The English in the Twelfth Century. Imperialism, National Identity and Political Values* (Woodbridge, The Boydell Press, 2000).

Klausner, David (ed.), *Wales, Records of Early Drama Series* (Toronto and London, University of Toronto Press and British Library, 2005).

Pryce, H., 'British or Welsh? National Identity in Twelfth-Century Wales', *English Historical Review*, 116 (2001), 775–801.

2 *Historia Regum Britanniae* and its sources

Bartrum, Peter C. (ed.), *Early Welsh Genealogical Tracts* (Cardiff: University of Wales Press, 1966).

——, *A Welsh Classical Dictionary. People in History and Legend up to about A.D. 1000* (Aberystwyth: National Library of Wales, 1993).

Dumville, D. N., 'The Historical Value of the *Historia Brittonum*', *Arthurian Literature*, 6 (1986), 1–26.

——, '*Historia Brittonum*: an Insular History from the Carolingian Age', in A. Scharer and G. Scheibelreiter (eds), *Historiographie im früheren Mittelalter* (Vienna: Oldenbourg, 1994), pp. 406–34.

Jones, G. and T. Jones (trans.), *The Mabinogion* (London: Everyman, 1949).

Le Duc, G., 'L'Historia Britannica avant Geoffroy de Monmouth', *Annales de Bretagne*, 79 (1982), 819–35.

Morris J. (ed. and trans.), *Nennius. British History and the Welsh Annals*, Arthurian Period Sources, vol. 8 (Chichester: Phillimore, 1980).

Owen, Morfydd, 'Royal Propaganda Stories from the Law-Texts', in Thomas Charles-Edwards, et al. (eds), *The Welsh King and his Court* (Cardiff: University of Wales Press, 2000), pp. 224–54.

Roberts, B., 'Geoffrey of Monmouth and Welsh Historical Tradition', *Nottingham Mediaeval Studies*, 20 (1976), 29–40.

Winterbottom, M. (ed. and trans.), *Gildas: The Ruin of Britain and Other Documents*, Arthurian Period Sources, vol. 7 (Chichester: Phillimore, 1978).

Wright, N., 'Geoffrey of Monmouth and Gildas', *Arthurian Literature*, 2 ([1982]), 1–40.

——, 'Geoffrey of Monmouth and Bede', *Arthurian Literature*, 6 (1986), 27–59.

3 Geoffrey's models: thinking about history in medieval Wales and Ireland

Byrne, Francis John, '*Senchas:* the Nature of Gaelic Historical Tradition', in J. G. Barry (ed.), *Historical Studies IX. Papers Read before the Irish Conference of Historians, Cork 29–31 May 1971* (Belfast: Blackstaff Press, 1974), pp. 137–59.

Carey, John, *A New Introduction to Lebor Gabála Érenn. The Book of the Taking of Ireland* (Dublin: Irish Texts Society, 1993).

Carey, John, *The Irish National Origin-Legend: Synthetic Pseudohistory,* Quiggin pamphlets on the sources of mediaeval Gaelic history (Cambridge, 1994).

——, *'Lebor Gabála* and the Legendary History of Ireland', in Helen Fulton (ed.), *Medieval Celtic Literature and Society* (Dublin: Four Courts Press, 2005), pp. 32–48.

Charles-Edwards, Thomas, 'The Arthur of History', in R. Bromwich, et al. (eds), *The Arthur of the Welsh* (Cardiff: University of Wales Press, 1991), pp. 15–32.

Coumert, Magali, *Origines des peuples: les récits du Haut Moyen Âge occidental (550–850)* (Paris: Institut d'Études Augustiniennes, 2007).

Hay, Denys, *Annalists and Historians. Western Historiography from the Eighth to the Eighteenth Centuries* (London: Methuen, 1977).

Macalister, R. A. S. (ed. and trans.), *Lebor Gabála Érenn. The Book of the Taking of Ireland,* 5 vols (rev. imprint, 1993; London: Irish Text Society, 1938–56).

Koch, John and John Carey (trans.), *The Celtic Heroic Age* (2nd edn; Andover, Mass.: Celtic Studies Publications, 1995).

Ó Corráin, D., 'Irish Origin Legends and Genealogy: Recurrent Aetiologies', in T. Nyberg, et al. (eds), *History and Heroic Tale: a Symposium* (Odense: Odense University Press, 1985), pp. 51–96.

——, 'Historical Need and Literary Narrative', in D. Ellis Evans (ed.), *Proceedings of the Seventh International Congress of Celtic Studies, Oxford, 1983* (Oxford: Oxford University Press, 1986), pp. 141–58.

——, 'Legend as Critic', in T. Dunne (ed.), *The Writer as Witness: Literature as Historical Evidence,* Historical Studies, 16 (Cork: Cork University Press, 1987), pp. 23–38.

——, 'Irish Vernacular Law and the Old Testament', in P. Ní Chatháin and M. Richter (eds), *Irland und die Christenheit. Ireland and Christendom* (Stuttgart: Klett-Cotta, 1987), pp. 284–307.

Scowcroft, R. Mark, *'Leabhar Gabhála* – Part I: the Growth of the Text', *Ériu,* 38 (1987), 81–142.

——, *'Leabhar Gabhála* – Part II: the Growth of the Tradition', *Ériu,* 39 (1988), 1–66.

Sims-Williams, P., 'Some Functions of Origin Stories in Early Medieval Wales', in T. Nyberg, et al. (eds), *History and Heroic Tale: a Symposium* (Odense: Odense University Press, 1985), pp. 97–131.

Thornton, D., 'Orality, Literacy and Genealogy in Early Medieval Ireland and Wales', in H. Pryce (ed.), *Literacy in Medieval Celtic Societies* (Cambridge: Cambridge University Press, 1998), pp. 83–98.

4 Geoffrey's Welsh inheritance: the red dragon and the promise of sovereignty

Bromwich, R. (ed), *Trioedd Ynys Prydein. The Welsh Triads* (3rd edn; Cardiff: University of Wales Press, 2006).

Lofmark, Carl, *A History of the Red Dragon*, ed. G. A. Wells (Llanrwst: Gwasg Carreg Gwalch, 1995).

Roberts, B. (ed.), *Cyfranc Lludd a Llefelys* (repr. 1995; Dublin: Dublin Institute for Advanced Studies, 1975).

5 Britain and Rome

Goffart, W., 'The Supposedly "Frankish" Table of Nations: an Edition and Study', in W. Goffart, *Rome's Fall and After* (repr. from *Frühmittelalterliche Studien*, 17 (1983), 98–130; London and Ronceverte: The Hambledon Press, 1989), pp. 133–65.

Jankulak, K., 'The Many-Layered Cult of St Caron of Tregaron', *Studia Celtica*, 41 (2007), 103–16.

6 Magnus Maximus and the colonization of Brittany

Casey, P. J., 'Magnus Maximus in Britain', in P. J. Casey (ed.), *The End of Roman Britain. Papers arising from a Conference, Durham, 1978* (London: BAR, 1979), pp. 66–79.

Dumville, D. N., 'Sub-Roman Britain: History and Legend', *History*, n.s. 62 (1977), 173–92; reprinted, with new material, in D. N. Dumville, *Histories and Pseudo-Histories of the Insular Middle Ages* (Aldershot: Variorum, 1990).

Jarrett, M. G., 'Magnus Maximus and the End of Roman Britain', *Transactions of the Honourable Society of Cymmrodorion* (1983), 22–35.

Matthews, J. F., 'Macsen, Maximus, and Constantine', *Welsh History Review*, 11 (1982/3), 431–48.

Roberts, B. (ed.), *Breudwyt Maxen Wledic* (Dublin: Dublin Institute for Advanced Studies, 2005).

——, '*Breuddwyd Maxen Wledig:* Why? When', in Joseph Falaky Nagy and Leslie Ellen Jones (eds), *Heroic Poets and Poetic Heroes in Celtic Tradition. A Festschrift for Patrick K. Ford. CSANA Yearbook 3–4* (Dublin: Four Courts Press, 2005), pp. 303–14.

7 The Arthurian section of *Historia Regum Britanniae*

Barber, R., 'Was Mordred Buried at Glastonbury? Arthurian Traditions at Glastonbury in the Middle Ages', *Arthurian Literature*, 4 (1985), 37–63.

Bromwich, R., et al. (eds), *The Arthur of the Welsh* (Cardiff: University of Wales Press, 1991).

Carley, James, 'Arthur in English History', in W. R. J. Barron (ed.), *The Arthur of the English* (Cardiff: University of Wales Press, 2001), pp. 47–57.

Lloyd-Morgan, Ceridwen, 'Welsh Tradition in Calais: Elis Gruffydd and his Biography of King Arthur', in Norris J. Lacy (ed.), *The Fortunes of King Arthur* (Cambridge: D. S. Brewer, 2005), pp. 77–91.

Padel, O.J., 'The Nature of Arthur', *Cambrian Medieval Celtic Studies*, 27 (1994), 1–31.

——, *Arthur in Medieval Welsh Literature*, Writers of Wales (Cardiff: University of Wales Press, 2000).

8 Merlin, *Prophetiae Merlini* and *Vita Merlini*

Bollard, John K., 'Myrddin in Early Welsh Tradition', in Peter Goodrich (ed.), *The Romance of Merlin: an Anthology* (New York and London: Garland, 1990), pp. 13–51.

Clarke, B. (ed. and trans.), *Life of Merlin. Geoffrey of Monmouth, Vita Merlini* (Cardiff: University of Wales Press, 1973).

Crick, Julia, 'Geoffrey of Monmouth, Prophecy and History', *Journal of Medieval History*, 18 (1992), 357–71.

Curley, Michael J., 'Animal Symbolism in the Prophecies of Merlin', in Willene B. Clark and Meradith T. McMunn (eds), *Beasts and Birds of the Middle Ages. The Bestiary and its Legacy* (Philadelphia, Pennsylvania: University of Pennsylvania Press, 1989), pp. 151–63.

—— (ed.), 'A New Edition of John of Cornwall's *Prophetia Merlini*', *Speculum*, 57 (1982), 217–49.

Daniels, Catherine, *Les prophéties de Merlin et la culture politique (Xiie-XVIe siècle)* (Turnhout: Brepols, 2006).

Davies, John Reuben, 'Bishop Kentigern among the Britons', in Steve Boardman, John Reuben Davies and Eila Williamson (eds), *Saints' Cults in the Celtic World* (Woodbridge: The Boydell Press, 2009), pp. 66–90.

Griffiths, Margaret Enid, *Early Vaticination in Welsh with English Parallels*, ed. T. Gwynn Jones (Cardiff: University of Wales Press, 1937).

Jarman, A. O. H., *The Legend of Merlin* (repr. 1976; Cardiff: University of Wales Press, 1960).

——, 'Early Stages in the Development of the Myrddin Legend', in Rachel Bromwich and R. Brinley Jones (eds), *Astudiaethau ar yr Hengerdd. Studies in Old Welsh Poetry* (Cardiff: University of Wales Press, 1978), pp. 326–49.

——, 'The Merlin Legend and the Welsh Tradition of Prophecy', in R. Bromwich, et al. (eds), *The Arthur of the Welsh* (Cardiff: University of Wales Press, 1991), pp. 117–45.

Padel, O. J., 'Geoffrey of Monmouth and the Development of the Merlin Legend', *Cambrian Medieval Celtic Studies*, 51 (2006), 37–65.

Roberts, B., 'Gerald of Wales and Welsh Tradition', in F. Le Saux (ed.), *The Formation of Culture in Medieval Britain* (New York, Queenston, Ontario, Lampeter: Edwin Mellen Press, 1995), pp. 129–47.

Scott, A. B. and F. X. Martin (ed. and trans.), *Expugnatio Hibernica. The Conquest of Ireland by Giraldus Cambrensis* (Dublin: Royal Irish Academy, 1978).

Thorpe, Lewis (trans.), *Gerald of Wales. The Journey through Wales. The Description of Wales* (Harmondsworth: Penguin, 1978).

Williams, Ifor (ed.) and R. Bromwich (trans.), *Armes Prydein. The Prophecy of Britain from the Book of Taliesin* (Dublin: Dublin Institute for Advanced Studies, 1982).

9 Welsh tradition and Geoffrey's legacy

Brennan, John P., 'Rebirth of a Nation? Historical Mythmaking in Layamon's *Brut*', in Allen J. Frantzen (ed.), *Essays in Medieval Studies 17: the Uses of the Past* (Morgantown, West Virginia: West Virginia University Press, 2000), pp. 19–29.

Crawford, T. D., 'On the Linguistic Competence of Geoffrey of Monmouth', *Medium Ævum*, 51 (1982), 152–62.

Crick, J., 'The British Past and the Welsh Future: Gerald of Wales, Geoffrey of Monmouth and Arthur of Britain', *Celtica*, 23 (1999), 60–75.

Ker, Neil R., 'Sir John Prise', *The Library*, 5th ser. 10 (1955), 1–24.

Lewis, Henry (ed.), *Brut Dingestow* (Cardiff: University of Wales Press, 1942).

Parry, J. J. (ed. and trans.), *Brut y Brenhinedd. Cotton Cleopatra Version* (Cambridge, Mass.: Medieval Academy of America, 1937).

Roberts, B., 'The Treatment of Personal Names in the Early Welsh Versions of *Historia Regum Britanniae*', *Bulletin of the Board of Celtic Studies*, 25 (1972–4), 274–90.

—— (ed.), *Brut y Brenhinedd. Llanstephan Ms. 1 Version* (Dublin: Dublin Institute for Advanced Studies, 1971).

Weiss, Judith (ed. and trans.), *Wace's Roman de Brut. A History of the British* (rev. edn; Exeter: University of Exeter Press, 2002).

Index